Wisdom
for a Lifetime

Wisdom for a Lifetime

How to Get the Bible Off the Shelf and Into Your Hands

Alden Studebaker

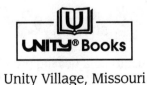

UNITY® Books

Unity Village, Missouri

First Edition 1998

Unity Books acknowledges these contributors to this book: Michael Maday, Brenda Markle, Raymond Teague, Sandy Price, Cathy McKittrick, editorial; Kay Thomure, copyediting; Shari Behr, Deborah Dribben, proofreading; Rozanne Devine, production; Diane Marshall, book design; Allen Liles, Sharon Sartin, Terri Springer, and Karen King, marketing.

To receive a catalog of all our Unity publications (books, cassettes, compact discs, and magazines) or to place an order, call our Customer Service Department: (816) 969-2069 or 1-800-669-0282.

Cover illustration by Joe Breeden

Cover design by Diane Marshall

The New Revised Standard Version is used for all Bible verses unless otherwise noted. Excerpts from the New Revised Standard Version and the American Standard Version Bibles are used by permission of the Division of Christian Education of the National Council of the Churches of Christ in the United States of America.

Scripture quotations marked "NKJV" are taken from the New King James Version. Copyright © 1979, 1980, 1982 by Thomas Nelson, Inc. Used by permission. All rights reserved. (Permissions continued on Permissions page.)

Library of Congress Cataloging-in-Publication Data

Studebaker, Alden, 1957–
    Wisdom for a lifetime : a handbook for getting the Bible off the shelf and into your hands / by Alden Studebaker.
        p.   cm.
    Includes bibliographical references and index.
    ISBN 0-87159-206-1
    1. Bible—Study and teaching. 2. Spiritual life—Unity School of Christianity.
    I. Title
    BS592.S78   1998
    220'.071—dc21   97-29960
                                                                      CIP

Dedication

This book is dedicated to my family, especially to my wife, Donna Studebaker, who believed in my ability to write when I doubted myself. Also, to my children, Jennifer, Nathan, and Danny, for their patience in enduring my ranting and raving in the midst of creative inspiration. ✏

Acknowledgments

I would like to acknowledge the following people and organizations for their positive, supportive influence upon the writing of this book:

Donna Studebaker, my proofreader and assistant

Roy Eugene Davis, my writing mentor and coach

Frank Giudici and **Warren Meyer** for reviewing the final manuscript and offering their suggestions

Gordon-Michael Scallion, who taught me to trust my own intuition

Michael Maday, Unity Books editor

Laura Barrett, **Donald Crooks**, **Judith Crooks**, **Karen Lindvig**, **Henry Studebaker**, and **Steve Towles** for reading each chapter as it was finished

Joseph Della Sorte, **Einar Denstad**, **Margaret Denstad**, **Donald Mattison**, and **Warren Meyer** for their prayerful support

Guntram Bischoff, **Elizabeth Giedeman**, **Otto Grundler**, **George Osmun**, my professors from Western Michigan University

Tim Allen, star of television's *Home Improvement,* and fellow Western Michigan alum, for unknowingly giving me the idea for the Bible study tool kit

Bob and **Robyn Clink** for providing our family with a house to live in at a reasonable cost during the writing of the book, and for some wonderful dinners, parties, and boys' nights out at the movies

Topeka Public Library and **Washburn University Library** that provided all the reference books I needed in researching the book

To my congregation, Garden Park Unity Church, Cincinnati, Ohio, for giving me the extra time to finish the final chapters ❧

Table of Contents

Part 1.
Why Read the Bible?

Chapter 1

The Purpose
of This Book

When we read a spiritually oriented book, we do so because it helps us open the doors to the experience of the divine within us. We feel an inner resonance with the message conveyed through the words the writer has assembled. It is as if we are the tourists and the book is our tour guide to more expansive states of consciousness.

We all have our favorite books of this kind and refer to them whenever we wish to reacquaint ourselves with certain spiritual concepts and perceptions. The readability of these books is often what attracts us to them. One can pick up such a book and almost instantly comprehend the meaning of the words without strenuous effort. Their user-friendliness continues to draw us back to them time and time again.

Another feature of these books is that the subject matter is relevant to our lives. It speaks to the issues that we consider important. For instance, if we are working on improving our self-image, then we might find ourselves reading books such as *Psycho-Cybernetics* and the like. However, if improving our self-image is not on our agenda, then we will likely be drawn to books that address topics of greater interest to us. If a book is germane to our place on the spiritual path, we will be attracted to that book and read it with much enthusiasm.

Of all the spiritual books available, the Bible is the most popular. In fact, the Bible is the most published book in history. Two significant events have led to this lofty status. The first was the invention of the printing press by Johannes Gutenberg of Mainz, Germany, in the fifteenth century. Prior to the advent of the printing press with its moveable type, books had to be produced by hand.

Scribes were employed for this labor-intensive procedure, one that was slow and tedious, and thus limited the number of books published. High cost and limited availability restricted book ownership to only the very rich and the religious elite. The printing press changed forever the exclusivity of book ownership. By 1501, nearly sixty years after its invention, over one thousand printing offices had published approximately thirty-five thousand different books with nearly ten million copies.[1] In 1515 the Fifth Lateran Council issued a decree forbidding the printing of books without the permission of the Roman Catholic leadership. We can now see that their attempts to control book production were entirely futile.

> **"Even though you intended to do harm to me, God intended it for good."**
> —Genesis 50:20

In 1455 Gutenberg and his first partner, Johann Fust, printed the first Bible, known today as the Gutenberg Bible. It is estimated that around two hundred were printed in this first edition though only forty-five are known to be extant. A number of these Bibles are located in the United States, namely at the Library of Congress, New York City Public Library, Pierpont Morgan Library, Harvard University, Yale University, and the Huntington Library in San Marino, California.

The text of the Gutenberg Bible was the Latin Vulgate, translated by St. Jerome around 400 c.e.[2] Although other translations of the Bible did exist in languages other than Latin, the Vulgate was the prevailing one. However, with the breakthrough of the printing press and the discovery of more ancient manuscripts, its predominance diminished. In 1466 Johann Mentel of Strasbourg printed a German language Bible. By the beginning of the sixteenth century, French, English, Italian, Dutch, and other vernacular European translations emerged. The best-known English translation, the King James Version commissioned by James I in 1604, was first published in 1611. We can readily see that the Gutenberg Bible was the parent of every Bible printed thereafter with copies now numbering in the billions.

The second most significant event leading to the propagation of the Bible was the Protestant Reformation of the sixteenth century. Led by Martin Luther and John Calvin, both Bible scholars in their own right, the Reformation professed that the Word of God came through the Scriptures and not necessarily from ecclesiastical authority. In the eyes of the reformers, spiritual belief and practice had to be supported with biblical Truth. By 1534 Luther himself had translated the Bible into his native German.

> "I will look with favor upon you and make you fruitful and multiply you; and I will maintain my covenant with you."
> —Leviticus 26:9

The advocating of biblical authority by the Protestant Reformation, combined with the technology of the printing press, opened up the reading of the Bible to the masses rather than the few and helped to propel the Bible into the first-place position it enjoys today. Today nearly every hotel room in America has a Gideon Bible available to its guests. All of which leads us to the purpose of this book.

When we consider the hotel Bible, the family Bible, the graduation Bible, whatever Bible, how often is the Bible read by the majority of Christians? When was the last time you actually sat down and read some verses of Scripture?

The current generation of people are, for the most part, unchurched and, therefore, un-Bibled. We have become a Bible-illiterate society. Many do not know the content of even the most basic Bible stories or the names of important Bible characters. For instance: Who was the father of the Hebrew people? What event led them to the Promised Land? Who fought the battle of Jericho? Who walked with Jesus on the water? Where was Paul going when he experienced his conversion? Because of this lack of Bible experience, there are a considerable number of people who have missed out on the spiritual Truth revealed through the stories, people, and passages in the Bible. They are unaware of these literary roots of spiritual support available to help ground, guide, and uplift them.

Metaphysical Christians[3] are among those whose Bible proficiency tends to be wanting. Since most have come from other churches, their aptitude for understanding Scripture is primarily dependent upon the nature of their prior religious background. Those with a mainline Protestant or fundamentalist background as a rule have adequate Bible skills. Former Roman Catholics generally are less endowed biblically. Non-Christians and those with the least religious exposure lag behind the former groups.

> **"The Lord bless you and keep you; the Lord make his face to shine upon you, and be gracious to you; the Lord lift up his countenance upon you, and give you peace."**
>
> —Numbers 6:24–26

Another reason for the deficiency in Bible knowledge among metaphysical Christians is simply the lack of studying the Bible. To many, Bible study is seen as a long and demanding task. They like hearing the Bible read from the pulpit but do not have the devotion nor the patience to study it themselves. They would rather read an easier book and leave the Bible study to ministers and teachers. Of those who do take a stab at reading the Bible, many often bog down along the way and give up.

This leads us to the point expressed earlier in this chapter. Spiritual books that are read are those which are easy to read and particularly of interest to the reader. Books that do not meet this criteria remain on the shelf gathering dust.

The Bible is often perceived as falling into the category of difficult-to-read books. First, it is a very long book with over a thousand pages. For most of us, reading any book with a thousand or more pages is a real drudge. Only James Michener seemed to be able to get away with writing books of this length. Second, the Bible was written for and about people who lived hundreds of years ago and, therefore, could not possibly be relevant to modern life. And so, who has time to read a thousand-page book written about people who have been dead and gone for centuries?

We can see that it is not too difficult to make a legitimate case for ignoring the Bible. With the limited study time available to modern people and the accessibility of so many other worthwhile spiritual books, it is no wonder that the Bible is overlooked by most metaphysical Christians. We might say to ourselves, "I'd like to study the Bible more than I do, but I'm just too busy." Unfortunately, this mentality has caused too many people to pass over the Bible in favor of other books, thus burying in a mental tomb of indifference any potential spiritual blessings that might be derived from biblical inquiry.

So, why this book? Is it actually possible to rekindle interest in the Bible? Can the Bible be made more readable and relevant? The answer is a definite *yes*. Even though the Bible is gathering dust on the bookshelves of most metaphysical Christians, with the right effort, it can be utilized as a powerful tool in the unfolding advancement of one's spiritual life. The initial aim of this book is to assist you, the potential Bible student, in overcoming the greatest hindrances to Bible study, its readability and relevancy. Once these hurdles are surmounted, a desire, an eagerness for biblical knowledge, will likely emerge. The Bible will no longer be viewed as an impossible Mount Everest, but rather as a vital component of one's spiritual sustenance.

There have been many fine books published on Bible interpretation. Each has imparted practical, spiritual insights into the passages they have covered. However, they have all neglected to explain how to actually do interpretation. *Wisdom for a Lifetime* seeks to fill this void. We have all heard the saying, "Give a man a fish; he eats for a day. Teach him how to fish; he eats for a lifetime." This book is like a fishing manual. It is your guide and partner, sometimes suggesting that you "cast the net on the right side of the boat"[4] in order to yield a greater abundance of spiritual food. Although it includes some examples of Bible interpretation, it is not intended to be a book of interpretations. Interpretations that have the greatest meaning and personal impact are always the kind that unfold from within ourselves.

Success in any endeavor often lies in knowing what kind of effort to make. This clearly applies to our quest for biblical Truth. Knowing how to apply oneself can make the difference between gaining usable ideas from the Bible and giving up in frustration. Some Truth is easily apprehended. Some Truth requires more elbow grease. If we desire to have the Bible reveal its spiritual potency, we must be willing to put forth the appropriate and sufficient effort. The purpose of this book is to offer suggestions as to how and where to place your efforts.

> **"You shall love the Lord your God with all your heart, and with all your soul, and with all your might."**
> —Deuteronomy 6:5

My motivation for writing *Wisdom for a Lifetime* is born out of a desire to help others such as myself, those with very little early biblical exposure. It was not until I attended college that my professors helped me discover the vast and profound world of the Bible. I feel I have been playing catch-up ever since. Through my experience as a Bible student and field minister, I have discovered a practical, workable approach to the Bible that continues to bless me with new insights and spiritual food.

Although every effort has been made to make *Wisdom for a Lifetime* scholastically correct, it is not written for biblical scholars and experts, but rather for those who have little or no Bible background. It is meant to be a companion to your Bible, your guide, your fishing manual. Its purpose is to assist you in reading, deciphering, understanding, and gaining meaningful spiritual benefit from your Bible and to keep it from wasting away on your bookshelf. The book is presented in three parts:

Part I, "Why Read the Bible?" explores the rewards of Bible study. Chapter 1, "The Purpose of This Book" (this chapter), introduces the prominence of the Bible in the literary world and outlines the primary obstacles many of us have toward Bible study. Chapter 2, "The Bible Is Not a Book," explains the process by which the Bible was written and the problems it creates in reading the Bible. Chapter 3, "The Sacredness of Scripture," delves into the importance of Scripture in religion. Chapter 4, "Metaphysical Christianity's Biblical Heritage," explains the uniqueness of the metaphysical approach toward the Bible and chronicles the many people who contributed toward this viewpoint.

> **"Where you go, I will go; Where you lodge, I will lodge; your people shall be my people, and your God my God."**
>
> —Ruth 1:16

Part II, "Assembling the Tools of Bible Study," outlines the use of the numerous resources available to the Bible student. Chapter 5, "Getting Started," describes the English translations currently available. Chapter 6, "Making a Bible Study Tool Kit," explains the function of Bible concordances, dictionaries, commentaries, atlases, and handbooks in Bible study. Chapter 7, "Close to the Source," shows how biblical knowledge can be enhanced by a familiarity with the Bible's original languages.

Part III, "Interpreting the Bible for Spiritual Growth," suggests methods of deriving practical benefit from Bible study. Chapter 8, "Everyone Interprets the Bible," reveals the many levels at which we interpret the Bible and life in general. Chapter 9, "The Uniqueness of Metaphysical Interpretation," demonstrates how to perform basic metaphysical Bible interpretation. Chapter 10, "Obtaining the Most From Your Bible," focuses on relating the Bible to specific personal needs and offers additional tips for succeeding at Bible study.

Finally, *Wisdom for a Lifetime* also includes a list of positive Bible passages from every book of the Bible, a bibliography, a glossary, and a topical index. Samplings of these Bible quotations are sprinkled throughout the text. They do not directly relate to the chapter material but rather provide a biblical backdrop—local color, as it were. And now, move on to the next chapter to discover why your Bible has been sitting on the shelf rather than being read.

Notes

1. Statistics reprinted with the permission of Simon & Schuster from *The Timetables of History* by Bernard Grun and Wener Stein. Copyright ©1946, 1963 by F. A. Herbig Verlagsbuchhandlung. English Language Edition copyright © 1975, 1979, 1991 by Simon & Schuster, Inc.

2. C.E. means Common or Christian Era, and replaces A.D. (Anno Domini), just as B.C.E. or Before the Common Era replaces B.C. (Before Christ).

3. The term *metaphysical Christian* generally encompasses people who participate in Unity, Religious Science, New Thought, and other progressive spiritual movements. The term *metaphysical* is defined in many ways by dictionaries. The way it is used throughout this book is explained in chapters 4, 8, and 9 and is not to be confused with the classic definition of *metaphysical* or *metaphysics,* which refers to a branch of philosophy that encompasses ontology, cosmology, and epistemology.

4. John 21:6, NKJV.

Chapter 2

The Bible
Is Not a Book

T he writing of books is a creative process of consciously bringing together ideas in an understandable form. Books have words, paragraphs, and chapters, each leading to another connected by a thread of thought that ultimately reaches a climax or conclusion. Most books have one author who knows the direction he or she wishes to take the reader. Some books have two or more authors who collaborate in the writing of a book (i.e., *The Quest,* written by Richard and Mary-Alice Jafolla). But most have one author, as in the case of this book. Books are generally written all at once, though some may be written over a period of several years. The process, if written by one author, obviously does not exceed that person's life-time. Additionally, nearly all books are written in one language, though they may later be translated into other languages to expand the reading audience. Many of these factors help contribute to making books both publishable and readable.

Consider the popularity of books such as *The Quest* and *A Course in Miracles* within the metaphysical arena. A survey of most Unity churches will reveal that there are more groups and classes studying these books than there are those studying the Bible. Why are people attracted to these books? What makes them more desirable to the reader than the Bible? The answer is fairly simple. *The Quest* and *A Course in Miracles,* unlike the Bible, are relatively easy to read. They read like books because they are books, albeit a channeled book in the case of *A Course in Miracles.*[1] Their authors present interesting, understandable ideas in a logical, purposeful sequence of chapters all in one language—many of the criteria of successful book writing.

Ironically, none of these aspects of literature apply to the best-selling book of all time, the Holy Bible. Why? Because the Bible is not a book. No, the Bible is not a book. The word *Bible* comes from the Greek *ta biblia* meaning "the books." The Bible is a collection of over sixty books written over thousands of years by an unknown number of authors with a diversity of intents and purposes, in two entirely different languages—neither of which is English! It is because of this unusual literary process that the Bible presents unique challenges to its readers.

> **"Go, do all that you have in mind; for the Lord is with you."**
> —2 Samuel 7:3

In some religious circles, the Bible's heterogeneous nature is not a substantial issue. The Bible is read because it is considered to be the absolute, irrefutable Word of God. God is the author and, therefore, whatever is in the Bible must be the undeniable Truth. If you want to know what God thinks on a certain matter, it's in the Bible. Dire consequences await those who ignore or defy the dictates of Scripture. Because of this sense of religious obligation, these Bible readers usually blind themselves to the Bible's distinctive complexity. There are even some who unconsciously and ignorantly believe that the Bible was actually written by God in our own language: English. To suggest that God did not come down from heaven in 1611 and write the King James Bible is a radical thought if not downright heresy. For these people, the Bible has become a "graven image"[2] to be worshiped with obsessive zeal.

This parochial inclination toward Bible study has sent many a metaphysical Christian searching for spiritual Truth in books other than the Bible. The thought of attending a Bible study group sends shivers of apprehension up the spine of many for fear of someone else's vain attempts to convert them to a narrow and overly simplistic belief about the Bible, God, and Jesus Christ. The Bible is frequently viewed as a book mainly for "Bible thumpers" and not for enlightened, progressive spiritual seekers.

Unfortunately for us modern folk, the Bible was never intended to be read as a spiritual guide the way *The Quest* and *A Course in Miracles* are. The purpose of these books is to aid the spiritual seeker in gaining personal, spiritual insight and guidance on a daily basis. All three books contain spiritual ideas. However, *The Quest* and *A Course in Miracles* are just easier to read and use. As previously mentioned, the Bible does not read like most spiritual books because it is not a book, but an anthology of books, letters, songs, poetry, lists, regulations, stories, sayings, and so forth. It seems like a chaotic collection from a reader's point of view, but it is the best possible one considering the complicated and ancient nature of the material. Let us examine this complexity in order to better understand exactly what we are facing when we pick up the Bible. How was the Bible written? What distinguishes it from other books? If God didn't write it, then who did?

The Bible is inspired writing. God may be the source of the ideas in the Bible, but humans are the writers, the channels through which these ideas are translated into words. As mentioned before, this is inspired writing. It's not that God is absent from the writing process, but there is always a human element and dimension to consider in the Bible.

Old Testament

Recall the one time in the Bible when God actually did do some writing of His own, so to speak. Moses went up to the top of Mount Sinai and received the Ten Commandments on tablets that had been "written with the finger of God."[3] It is a matter of conjecture whether God used Moses as a recording secretary for this first set of tablets. The first mention of the Ten Commandments was a verbal recounting of them by Moses to the Israelite nation. Anyway, while Moses was still on the mountain, he discovered that the people had forged themselves a golden calf, a clear violation of the "thou shalt not make unto thee any graven image"[4] statute they had received weeks earlier from Moses. After some skillful plea bargaining on the part of Moses in which he convinced God that retribution against the whole of the Israelite people was not in His best interests, Moses returned from his journey up the mountain. As he entered the Israelite camp, he became so enraged by their dancing around the golden calf that he threw the tablets on the ground breaking them to pieces. Later, God, with the help of Moses, made a replacement set of tablets.

As we look at this story about the serious and important writing of the Ten Commandments, we can see an amusing situation emerge. Moses, one of the most respected figures in the Bible, in a fit of rage, trashed the first set of manuscripts that God had produced. Even when God tried to do some writing of the Bible, He had to deal with human beings and their foibles. And, when the second set of tablets was made, the commandments on these were not identical to the first ones. What had happened? Had God changed His mind? Did Moses alter the new tablets? Or is there more to this than meets the eye? Perhaps so. One conclusion we can make is that we cannot underestimate the human quotient when reading the Bible. That is, *people* wrote the Bible.

> **"As the Lord lives, whatever the Lord says to me, that I will speak."**
> —1 Kings 22:14

Back to the question, Is there more to these passages than meets the eye? Certainly. Bible passages may appear contradictory, illogical, and perplexing. When contradictions and inconsistencies arise in the study of Scripture, serious Bible students cannot dismiss these oddities as unimportant. The causes of these anomalies are often found in the unusual manner by which the Bible came to be written. In the case of the two sets of Ten Commandments, the answer lies in the literary roots of each set, roots that differ in origin.

According to most scholars, the first five books[5] of the Old Testament or Hebrew Bible have four principal, identifiable literary sources. Scholars are today talking about an "R" source, but R was more of an editor than a writer. These materials are generally categorized as the J, E, D, and P writers. What appears to be alphabet soup are actually the scholastic names for the various writers and editors of the Old Testament, each one exerting a certain influence on the finished product.

The J writer,[6] known as the Jahwist, used the Hebrew word *Yahweh* when referring to God. *Jehovah,* the familiar name for God, is a derivation of *Yahweh.* The J writer, the earliest of the four writers, lived in the southern kingdom of Judah about 950 B.C.E.

The E writer, or Elohist, chose the word *Elohim* for God. Many Hebrew names and name places have the word *El* in them, connecting them to a particular aspect of God. For example, *Elisha* means "whom God is salvation"; *Bethel* means "house of God." The E writer came from the northern kingdom of Israel and had his influence on the Bible circa 850 B.C.E.

The D writer, known as the Deuteronomic Historian, came into the picture during the reforms of Josiah, king of Judah, in 621 B.C.E. This writer's main interest centered on the restoration of and adherence to religious law. Much of the book of Deuteronomy, from which the writer receives his name, was composed by the D writer.

Last, but not least, we have P, the Priestly Writer. This literary source emerged from among the priesthood during the Babylonian exile around 550 B.C.E. Concerned with rituals, regulations, and traditions, the book of Leviticus is a prime example of the P writer.

An oral tradition of legends, myths, and stories, as exists in all cultures, naturally preceded the JEDP writers and provided a foundation from which they built their ideas. This oral tradition, the JEDP writers, and other less identifiable sources together comprised the material in the Pentateuch, which was compiled in its finalized form at the time of Ezra, around 400 B.C.E. The influence of the JEDP writers also extended into many other books of the Old Testament, namely Joshua, Judges, 1 & 2 Samuel, and 1 & 2 Kings.

Now, let us return to the two versions of the Ten Commandments. According to biblical scholarship, the first version is considered to be a P edition of the original commandments and the second version a predominantly J document. And, as if two versions weren't enough, a third Ten Commandments[7] is found in the book of Deuteronomy, which is considered to be an entirely D document.

> **"Seek the Lord and his strength, seek his presence continually."**
> —1 Chronicles 16:11

Another classic example of the multiple sources of Bible literature is found in the opening chapters of the book of Genesis, the story of creation or, in this case, the *stories* of creation. Read Genesis 1:1—2:4. God creates the world in six days and takes a break on the seventh day. Read Genesis 2:5—3:24. Bam! Here's another story of creation with Adam, Eve, God, and the serpent—a full cast of characters. Which story is the authentic one? The second story seems to grow out of the first, almost as if it were planned that way. However, there are numerous contradictions between them. For instance, man and woman had already been created in the first story, and yet they are created again in the second account. Additionally, the first story tells of the fruit trees and herbs available to man for food. The second story begins by saying, "before any plant of the field was in the earth and before any herb of the field had grown."[8]

As in the case of the Ten Commandments, the reason for these multiple creation stories is rooted in their literary lineage.

To the casual reader, it appears that the first creation story is probably the most ancient, with the second one having been written later. Yet the very opposite is true. Our friend the P writer wrote the first story hundreds of years after the J writer crafted the second story.

Look further ahead in the Old Testament to the book of Isaiah. At first glance, this book appears to be written by the prophet himself. Indeed, scholars consider Isaiah to be one of the great literary prophets and the probable writer of much of the book. Even the title of the book somewhat implies that there is just one writer. However, upon a closer examination of its content and writing style, scholars have identified two other distinguishable writers of the book of Isaiah. Who are these different Isaiahs? Will the real Prophet Isaiah please stand up!

First, Chapters 1–39 are the work of the original Prophet Isaiah, who lived during the latter part of the eighth century B.C.E. Known as First Isaiah, he warned the people of their impending destruction. His ministry spanned the reign of four kings of the southern kingdom of Judah.

Chapters 40–55 are the work of an unknown writer who, based on the content of his writing, lived during the period of the Babylonian exile (587– 539 B.C.E.), possibly in Babylon itself. Known as Second Isaiah,[9] his message was one of hope for the future of the Jewish exiles and their ultimate return to Palestine.

The final chapters of the book of Isaiah (56–66) reveal a Third Isaiah.[10] His writing was directed toward the postexilic community in Palestine working to rebuild their lives following the upset and turmoil of the Exile. Thus Third Isaiah wrote during the period after 538 B.C.E.

So we have three Isaiahs, two creation stories, and four Ten Commandments. What's a reader to think? Which version is more genuine than the other? Why does everything in the Bible seem to be put together like a tossed salad? Have too many cooks spoiled the soup? What is the purpose in having such a diversity of story line and authorship?

The key to understanding this unusual writing method has to do with the mind-set of the compilers of the biblical writings. We have all heard the phrase *they threw in everything but the kitchen sink,* alluding to someone who has included nearly everything possible and more in assembling needed items for a project, trip, or food dish. The writers and editors of the Bible, especially in the Old Testament, took the kitchen sink approach. If a story or writer had some validity or importance to the overall message of Judaism, it was included and accommodated in the text of the Scriptures. As you read through the Old Testament, you will notice many instances of multiple stories, conflicting ideas, and stilted writing—the direct result of this all-inclusive editorial approach, one that makes the text difficult to read.

> **"The battle is not yours but God's."**
> —2 Chronicles 20:15

By the time the Old Testament was written, compiled, edited, and authorized, it comprised some thirty-nine[11] books. These books were separated into three sections: The Torah or Books of Moses: Genesis through Deuteronomy; The Prophets: Joshua through 2 Kings, Isaiah, Jeremiah, Ezekiel, plus the Twelve minor prophets; and The Writings: All other books including Psalms, Proverbs, Job, and Daniel just to name a few.

New Testament

The New Testament, like the Old Testament, is also a compilation of various writings by numerous authors—twenty-seven books in all. Each book was written with a specific purpose in mind; for instance, the Gospels were written to get the word out to the people about the wondrous works and teachings of Jesus Christ. The Acts of the Apostles, a continuation of the gospel of Luke, chronicles the history of the early Christian church. Paul's epistles were essentially letters of support to the various churches around the ancient world, letters much like the kind we write today. Certainly, Paul did not expect that these letters would be published for us to read thousands of years later. And the last book of the Bible, the book of Revelation, written by an unknown author in the latter part of the first century C.E., directed a message of hope toward Jewish Christians living in the Roman Empire.

The New Testament, when compared with the Old Testament, is much more readable. Christians, and especially metaphysical Christians, read the New Testament far more often than the Old Testament. A number of factors have led to this special attraction: One, Jesus Christ, the central figure of the New Testament, is a universal hero.

> **"The joy of the Lord is your strength."**
> —Nehemiah 8:10

His teachings are for anyone regardless of ethnic background. The primary focus of the Old Testament centers on God and His relationship to the Israelite people, consequently excluding to some extent anyone who is not Jewish.

Two, the New Testament was written in an ancient form of Greek.[12] Due to the achievements of Alexander the Great, Greek became the language of the ancient world, as is English today. It was only natural for the New Testament writers, especially the Gospel writers, to choose Greek as the language of their efforts. Greek is a language from which English and other modern European languages have borrowed heavily in their development. For example, the English *three,* the Spanish *tres,* the German *drei,* and the French *trois* have much in common with the older Greek *treis.*

On the other hand, the Hebrew of the Old Testament is a Semitic language like Arabic. Consider the Hebrew *shalom* and the Arabic *salaam,* both words for peace. Hebrew as well as Arabic are not cognate with most modern European languages. This characteristic makes Hebrew much more difficult to translate into European languages than Greek. The congruity between Greek and many European languages—namely English—allows it to be more easily rendered in those languages.

And three, the New Testament is a more recent document, hence the name *New Testament*. The earliest writings in the New Testament are Paul's letters, written around 50–60 C.E. The earliest Old Testament writings (the J writer) come from around the time of King Solomon, 950 B.C.E., hundreds of years before Paul. Since fewer years have passed since its original writing, there is less chance for the New Testament to have been altered from its initial manuscripts.

Another time element to consider when comparing the writing of the New and Old Testaments is the span of time over which the materials were written. In the case of the New Testament, barely one hundred years were required versus the Old Testament's nearly eight hundred years.[13]

> "You will decide on a matter, and it will be established for you, and light will shine on your ways."
>
> —Job 22:28

Also, unlike the Old Testament, nearly every book of the New Testament was written by a singular author. Although each writer had to deal with multiple sources of information, much as a reporter would have to do today, the process was much less complex than with the Old Testament.[14] Do you remember the three Isaiahs? And, in the case of the gospel of Luke, its writer is also the author of the Acts of the Apostles.

It is fascinating to note how the degree of readability coincides with the basic parameters for successful book publishing mentioned earlier in this chapter. One possible exception to the readability issue is the book of Revelation, which actually belongs to the apocalyptic[15] genre of writings, much like its Old Testament cousins Daniel and Ezekiel.

Apocrypha and Pseudepigrapha

Thus far, if you're keeping count, the book tally for the Bible comes to a total of sixty-six; thirty-nine for the Old Testament, twenty-seven for the New Testament. While for most readers, sixty-six books is plenty to read, it is merely a subtotal. A vast number of other scriptural writings of both Jewish and Christian origin were composed and circulated, and some of them can be found in certain editions of the Bible. These books have sparked controversy and debate throughout the last 2000 years. They were either considered too advanced for the average reader or less authoritative and inspired than the rest of the Bible. These books are designated by various terms, depending upon the religious group consulted. Allow me to explain these books as accurately and simply as possible.

Let's begin with the Jewish writings. Between about 200 B.C.E.–100 C.E., a diverse collection of books, approximately fifteen in number, written predominantly in Greek, became widely read by both Jews and early Christians. Some of these books are connected to Old Testament books (i.e., 1 Esdras, Esther) others are freestanding books (i.e., Judith, Tobit, Wisdom of Solomon, and so forth). In 90 C.E., the Jewish Council of Jamnia finalized the Hebrew Bible into its accustomed form, leaving out these books. However, early Christians continued to embrace these writings. The Latin translation of the Bible, the Vulgate (see Chapter 1), includes many of these books. Beginning in the sixteenth century C.E., Protestants, interested in maintaining biblical purity, began excluding them from the Bible.

Today these books are generally referred to as the Apocrypha, meaning "hidden things." Catholic Bibles include some Apocryphal books. Most Protestant Bibles exclude the Apocrypha, although a few include it as a separate section between the Old and New Testaments. Most scholars consider the Apocryphal writings an important historical and literary link between the Old and New Testaments, often referring to them as Intertestamental books. I have included a few citations in this book (see Chapter 8 and Appendix B) to help pique your interest in studying the Apocrypha.

Another much larger group of Jewish writings from about

the same time period is loosely known as the Pseudepigrapha, meaning "writing under a false or assumed name." Some of these books were attributed to famous Old Testament characters such as Abraham and Moses. Other anonymously written books cannot be categorized as pseudepigraphal. Even though no books of the Pseudepigrapha are found in the Bible or in the Apocrypha, their importance lies in their influence upon New Testament writers. For example, the author of the book of Jude relied upon two of these books (The Assumption of Moses & 1 Enoch) in his writing.

Finally, many early and modern Christian writers have composed books not found in the Bible. These books are referred to as the Christian Apocrypha or the Apocryphal New Testament. Many appear to resemble New Testament writings by employing terms such as *gospel, epistle,* or *acts,* and attributing them to biblical characters

"Be still, and know that I am God!"

—Psalm 46:10

(i.e., Gospel of Thomas, Third Epistle to the Corinthians, Acts of Peter, and so on). The Nag Hammadi Library, a collection of early Gnostic Christian writings found in Egypt in 1945, are among this group. Examples of modern Apocrypha could include *The Aquarian Gospel* and *The Lost Books of the Bible.*

Summary

The point of all this detailed scholarly mumbo jumbo is that the Bible is clearly not the work of one, two, or even three writers, but an unknown number, possibly hundreds, each one possessing a particular outlook, style, and purpose. As hard as it is for us modern people to admit, there is just no way of knowing precisely who wrote the Bible. We take our best scholarly guess and leave the rest as a mystery not likely to be solved.

In addition, not only must we take into account the sources of biblical writing but the editing process as well. A good analogy of this procedure can be found in our own government. A bill is introduced in Congress. It is sent to subcommittees, committees, the House of Representatives, the Senate, and the President. If all goes well the bill becomes law. The original bill and the finished product may only slightly resemble each other. As careful as the biblical editors were, they were people and were, therefore, subject to expressing their unique opinions, biases, and objectives. Today, for better or worse, we are subject to their mark upon the Bible.

Let us continue to remember: God is the source of the ideas in the Bible, but people are the writers and editors of the words. One might say that if the Bible were a person it would have a *multiple personality,* but one which has been integrated to the best possible extent.

You might ask at this point, "How does this information make a difference to me today?" The answer is this: It is always helpful to know who the authors are of the words you are reading and to whom they are writing. In the case of the Bible, its authors were primarily writing for the people of their day. Yet, in the midst of the their single-minded purpose, a message of universal Truth has come through to each successive generation.

It is my hope that these samples of biblical literature have helped to paint a picture of the nature of Bible authorship. You may begin to see why we cannot expect the Bible to read like a book. What we can do is expect it to read like what it is: an accumulation of fascinating, powerful, and inspiring literature.

The difficulties encountered with the Bible should not preclude one from reading it. Keep in mind, Bible study cannot be hurried. There are no crash courses. It is something that requires consistent study, work, application on a regular basis, and overtime, as do other spiritual practices such as meditation, prayer, affirmations, or goal-setting. A certain degree of patience will pay off in big spiritual dividends. Look at the spiritual Truth one gains from, for instance, the creation stories, both of them. We learn of the divine origins of humanity and the process by which humanity cast itself into duality and materiality. Can we learn this same Truth more easily from other sources? Perhaps. However, Truth obtained through your own efforts in biblical study will remain with you throughout your life. The Bible has that kind of staying power.

In spite of all the barriers to reading the Bible, its peculiar and challenging authorship and its seemingly haphazard arrangement, when viewed as a whole, it appears to make sense. The beginning, middle, and end have a spiritual congruency that seems utterly miraculous, divine, holy.

Notes

1. Channeled books are those in which a disincarnate being writes through the vehicle of an embodied medium or *channel* by way of a process called automatic writing. Jesus Christ is claimed to be the author of *A Course in Miracles.*

2. Exodus 20:4, KJV.

3. Exodus 31:18, KJV. It is assumed that the tablets contained the Ten Commandments. See Deuteronomy 10:1–5.

4. Exodus 20:4, KJV.

5. Known as the *Pentateuch* (penta meaning five) or *The Books of Moses.* Tradition claims that Moses is the author of the Pentateuch. This is unlikely given current biblical scholarship and the fact that Moses would have had to have written about his own death (Deuteronomy 34:5).

6. The term *writer* refers to an unknown number of writers.

7. Deuteronomy 5:6–21. A watered-down fourth version is found in Leviticus 19:1–22.

8. Genesis 2:5, NKJV.

9. Also known as Deutero-Isaiah.

10. Also known as Trito-Isaiah.

11. Originally, the books of the Hebrew Bible numbered 24. Contemporary divisions and arrangements bring the number to 39.

12. Known as *Koine Greek,* it was similar to the Greek of Greece's Golden Age. *Koine Greek* was a commoner's language taken from the word *koinos,* meaning "common or general."

13. From the tenth century B.C.E. to the book of Daniel, around 165 B.C.E.

14. Scholars also use letters to describe the literary sources of the Gospels, much in the same way they use the letters J, E, D, and P to label Old Testament writers. Mark is considered to be the first Gospel, written around 70 C.E. He likely used a source referred to as Q, from the German word, *quelle,* meaning source. The writers of Matthew and Luke, aware of Mark's Gospel, and Q, likely also had access to their own unique sources labeled M and L. All of the Gospels and their sources had their origins in an oral tradition of first-hand accounts, stories, and legends.

15. Belonging to those prophetic writings describing the battle between good and evil and the ultimate triumph of good over evil.

Chapter 3

The Sacredness of Scripture

S criptures have played an integral role in the religions of the world since the beginning of humanity. Whether orally transmitted or written down, this revered literature has governed, guided, inspired, and directed the steps of people toward an experience of their innate spiritual nature. Scriptures communicate ideas—ideas considered to be extraordinary if not supernatural. Their words are imbued with authority and potency. We believe scripture to be sacred, bestowed with a divine or holy element. Writings included in the canon[1] of scripture are those distinguished as having this sacred quality. To put it a bit outrageously, there is no mistaking the Holy Bible for, say, the *National Enquirer* in the minds and hearts of most people!

Because of the veneration and respect people have for their scriptures, these writings have subsequently influenced the behavior of cultures in a significant way. For instance, the Jewish Passover festival is performed in commemoration of the final plague God visited upon the Egyptian people, the killing of all the firstborn—a pestilence that *passed over* the Hebrew households. This event ultimately led to the deliverance of the Hebrew people from centuries of enslavement at the hands of the Egyptians. During this weeklong celebration, participants eat unleavened bread[2] and perform other rites in remembrance of this ancient event. Refer to Exodus 11:1—12:30 for the historical background and religious instructions pertaining to Passover.

Consider the Bible's effect on the annual Sunday School Christmas pageant. Each person, animal, and element portrayed in the Christmas story[3] is painstakingly woven into the drama of the presentation. Boys play Joseph, Herod, Wise Men, the Innkeeper, and shepherds.

"Trust in the Lord with all your heart."
—Proverbs 3:5

Girls play Mary, angels, stable animals, and even a shepherd or two (there are not many parts specifically for girls). Parents, sitting in the audience, beam with pride and adoration as they watch their children perform.

In a court of law, the civic ritual of placing our hands on the Bible to swear that "what you are about to say is the whole truth and nothing but the truth so help you God" almost implies that the Bible has the power to make us tell the truth. Though we sophisticated modern folk may not easily admit it, scripture has always been a powerful force in society, from the Bible, to *The Book of Mormon,* to the *Koran.*

Some Christians ignorantly believe that the Bible is the only true scripture. To them, one could not possibly benefit from reading scriptures other than the Bible for, after all, the Bible is the final authority. All else is at the very least suspect, if not satanic in nature.

Metaphysical Christians have long discarded this narrow perspective and easily accept the validity of scriptures from other faiths. I highly encourage the reading of nonbiblical scriptures, for it helps free the mind from the restricting shackles of religious chauvinism and opens it up to an appreciation for other spiritual paths. Some have even explored these alternative scriptures, seeking new insights into their own spirituality. Unfortunately, in their quest for knowledge, metaphysical Christians have disregarded the Bible with nearly as much facility as puritanical Christians ignore the *Tao Te Ching.*

Speaking of the Tao Te Ching, let us enjoy these selections of scripture from the great world religions:

Hinduism

The oldest of the major world religions, Hinduism has the unique status of having no founding date, nor founder. The archaeological sites of Harappa and Mohenjo-daro in the Indus River Valley, dating back to before 3000 B.C.E., are the first-known locations of Hindu religion. Over the millennia, Hinduism has grown, been invaded, adapted, and evolved to endure as the dominant religion on the Indian subcontinent.

Hinduism contains hundreds of different scriptures, mostly written in Sanskrit. The *Vedas* are the most ancient of these writings and are considered the most authoritative. They originally existed in an oral tradition for centuries, meticulously passed down from teacher to pupil until they were rendered into written form around 800 B.C.E. The best-known books from the Vedas are the *Upanishads,* meaning "to sit near and listen." Here is an excerpt from the Chhandogya Upanishad:

"Now, the light which shines above this heaven, above all the worlds, above everything, in the highest worlds not excelled by any other worlds, that is the same light which is within man. There is this visible proof [of this light]: when we thus perceive by touch the warmth in the body. And of it we have this audible proof: when we thus hear, by covering the ears, what is like the rumbling of a carriage, or the bellowing of an ox, or the sound of a blazing fire. One should worship [as Brahman] that [inner] light which is seen and heard. He who knows this becomes conspicuous and celebrated, yea, he becomes celebrated."[4]

Compare this verse from the Upanishads with Genesis 1:1–4; Isaiah 60:1, 19–20; Daniel 5:14; Matthew 5:14–16; and Luke 11:33–36.

Perhaps the best known of the Hindu scriptures, the *Bhagavad Gita* or *The Lord's Song*, is but a small portion of a larger work known as the *Mahabharata*. The Mahabharata is perhaps the longest literary work in existence, an epic poem some 100,000 stanzas in length, many times longer than the Greek epics *The Iliad* and *The Odyssey* combined. From the sixteenth chapter of the Bhagavad Gita:

> *"The Lord said:* Fearlessness, purity of heart, steadfastness in knowledge and yoga; charity, self-control, and sacrifice; study of the scriptures, austerity, and uprightness;
>
> "Non-violence, truth, and freedom from anger; renunciation, tranquillity, and aversion to slander; compassion to beings and freedom from covetousness; gentleness, modesty, and absence of fickleness;
>
> "Courage, forgiveness, and fortitude; purity, and freedom from malice and overweening pride—these belong to him who is born with divine treasures. . . .
>
> "Ostentation, arrogance, and self-conceit; anger, rudeness, and ignorance—these belong to him who is born to the heritage of the demons. . . .
>
> "The divine treasures are said to be for the purpose of liberation, and the heritage of the demons, for bondage. Grieve not, O Pāndava; you are born with divine treasures.
>
> "There are two types of beings created in this world: the divine and the demoniac. The divine have been described at length. Hear now from Me, O Pārtha, concerning the demoniac. . . .

"Men of demoniac nature know not what to do and what to refrain from doing. Purity is not in them, nor good conduct, nor truth. . . .

"Giving themselves up to insatiable desires, full of hypocrisy, pride, and arrogance, they hold false views through delusion and act with impure resolve.

"Beset with innumerable cares, which will end only with death, looking on the gratification of desire as their highest goal, and feeling sure that this is all;

"Bound by a hundred ties of hope, given up wholly to lust and wrath, they strive, by unjust means, to amass wealth for the satisfaction of their passions. . . .

"He who discards the injunctions of the scriptures and acts upon the impulse of desire attains neither perfection nor happiness nor the Supreme Goal."[5]

Pick up your Bible! Look up Galatians 5:16–26. Do you notice the similarities between the two passages? What is the cause of these parallel ideas showing up in two entirely different writings? The Bhagavad Gita was written hundreds of years before Paul. Given the long distances between India and Paul's location somewhere in the Middle East (we do not know Paul's location when he wrote his letter to the Galatians), it is unlikely that he had a copy of it to read. Perhaps Paul became aware of these essential spiritual Truths through his own inner process. He wrote other like ideas in Colossians 3:5–16 and Philippians 4:8.

Buddhism

Like Hinduism, Buddhism began on the Indian subcontinent. Siddhartha Gautama, born around 560 B.C.E., was a

Hindu, a prince, and an heir to his father's throne. At twenty-nine, he left behind the luxury of the palace to find answers to life's questions. His quest for Truth led him to the experience of his own enlightenment. For forty years, the Buddha[6] taught throughout India until his death in 480 B.C.E. His experiences are well chronicled in Buddhist writings. Through its history, unlike Hinduism, Buddhism did not gain a permanent foothold in India but has drawn the bulk of its followers from Sri Lanka, Burma, Thailand, Indochina, China, and Japan.

The body of Buddhist scripture is immense and complex. It began, as other scriptures have, as an oral tradition. In the first century B.C.E., it was written down in Pali, a derivative language of Sanskrit. This first collection of writings is known as the Pali Canon. Many other scriptures were written in Chinese, Tibetan, and Sanskrit. The *Dhammapada*, a book from the Pali Canon, aptly describes the Buddhist spiritual path. Some translators of the book say that to read the Dhammapada is almost like hearing the Buddha himself speak. Here are the opening verses from the Dhammapada. As you read them, do they remind you of a certain passage from the Bible?[7]

> **"For everything there is a season, and a time for every matter under heaven."**
>
> —Ecclesiastes 3:1

"We are what we think,
  having become what we thought.
Like the wheel that follows the
    cart-pulling ox,
Sorrow follows an evil thought.

And joy follows a pure thought,
  like a shadow faithfully tailing a man.
We are what we think,
  having become what we thought."[8]

Taoism

Earlier in this chapter, reference was made to the Tao Te Ching. This writing, dating from the sixth century B.C.E., is probably the most recognized piece of literature from China and is the fundamental scripture of the mystical Taoist religion. Its name is difficult to translate into English and is simply rendered, *The Way.*

Legend states that Lao Tzu, an elderly man, weary over the corruption he witnessed in the royal court, left the city for the wilderness to die in peace. Upon reaching the city limits, the guard at the gate demanded that the philosopher write down his wisdom before he was allowed to pass. The result of his detention at the border was the Tao Te Ching. Here is Chapter 29:

"Do you think you can take over the universe
    and improve it?
I do not believe it can be done.

The universe is sacred.
You cannot improve it.
If you try to change it, you will ruin it.
If you try to hold it, you will lose it.

So sometimes things are ahead and sometimes
    they are behind;
Sometimes breathing is hard, sometimes it
    comes easily;
Sometimes there is strength and sometimes
    weakness;
Sometimes one is up and sometimes down.

Therefore the sage avoids extremes,
    excesses, and complacency."[9]

Confucianism

Like Taoism, Confucianism is indigenous to China. Where Taoism developed into a sectarian religious form, Confucianism's influence on the Chinese mind and practical daily life was far more extensive. Born in 551 B.C.E. in the Shantung Province, state of Lu, Confucius (a Latin version of his name is Kung Fu-tzu or Master Kung) was a younger contemporary of Lao Tzu. He is fabled to have consulted with Lao Tzu at one point in his life.

Concerned with the decline of government and its detrimental effects on the average person, Confucius focused much of his energy upon applying basic virtue to statesmanship. He even tried his hand at politics, serving as a high ranking official of the government. Though his efforts had a prosperous influence upon the state,

"There is no flaw in you."
—Song of Solomon 4:7

they were later thwarted when he resigned to protest the ruler's preoccupation with pleasure. Confucius spent the rest of his life traveling throughout China teaching his philosophy to his pupils and to other rulers. Although Confucius did not live to see his ideas fully implemented (as is so often the case with visionaries), his effect on China over the centuries has been profound.

The most significant scripture of Confucianism, *The Analects of Confucius*, are accepted as Confucius' own words. To play off the old joke, here is what Confucius says about personal virtue:

> "Those who lack moral virtue cannot abide long in a state either of poverty or pleasure. Those who possess moral virtue find their comfort therein. Those who are wise know the profit of virtue. . . .

> The princely man never for a single instant
> quits the path of virtue; in times of storm and
> stress he remains in it as fast as ever. . . .
>
> The wise man will be slow to speak but quick
> to act."[10]

It's time again to open your Bible. Pick any chapter from the book of Proverbs and read it. You may have noticed that the Tao Te Ching and The Analects of Confucius read very much like this Old Testament book.

Zoroastrianism

Though not regarded as a principal world religion, were it not for a change of historical destiny, Zoroastrianism might have become a much more significant player on the modern religious world scene. Zoroastrianism once was the predominant religion of ancient Persia.[11] The followers of the prophet, Zoroaster, now number only in the thousands.

Little concrete knowledge exists about Zoroaster (a Greek form of the Persian, Zarathustra). Tradition says that he was born of a virgin in the latter part of the seventh century B.C.E., rose to become a teacher, and eventually converted the ruler Vishtaspa to his spiritual principles. These principles included a belief in one God, called Ahura Mazda (Ahura means "Lord," Mazda means "wisdom"), the dualism of good and evil, the prevailing power of good, and a belief in an afterlife. The scriptures of Zoroastrianism are an aggregation of writings called the *Avesta,* written in a number of ancient Persian dialects over the centuries. Here is a selection from the Bundahis:

> "The first of Ahura Mazda's creatures of the
> world was the sky, and his good thought, by

good procedure, produced the light of the world, along with which was the good religion of the Mazdayasnians.

Of Ahura Mazda's creatures of the world, the first was the sky; the second, water; the third, earth; the fourth, plants; the fifth, animals; the sixth, mankind.

Ahura Mazda produced illumination between the sky and the earth, the constellation stars and those also not of the constellations, then the moon, and afterwards the sun."[12]

Quick! Whip out your Bible to the first chapter of the book of Genesis and read it. What do you think? Isn't it quite uncanny that Zoroastrian and Old Testament creation stories so closely resemble each other?

What about that twist of fate that has left Zoroastrianism nearly on the brink of extinction as a world religion? According to some scholars, if the Greeks had not defeated the Persian navy in the Battle of Salamis in 480 B.C.E., Zoroastrianism, not Christianity, would have likely become the prevailing religion of Europe and possibly America. It is interesting to speculate about such turning points in history. Anyway, to finish the story, the Persians left Greece a defeated nation and entered into a period of decline. So did their religion. Over a thousand years later, Zoroastrianism was nearly eradicated from Persia at the hands of the proselytizing Muslims, leaving its remaining followers to become refugees in India, where they are known today as Parsis (from the name *Persia*).

> **"Call to me and I will answer you, and will tell you great and hidden things that you have not known."**
>
> —Jeremiah 33:3

Zoroastrianism's influence on world religions and scripture is not limited to its present expression. The Jewish exiles in Babylon, having been liberated by Cyrus of Persia, were certainly exposed to Zoroastrian thought. In the Christmas story, the Wise Men from the East[13] were called *Magi,* a term referring to Zoroastrian priests.

Islam

Any study of the world's scriptures must include a visit to the sacred book of Islam, the *Qur'an* or *Koran.* This book, revealed through the prophet Muhammad, is perhaps among the least altered or edited of any scripture. Part of this purity resides in its youthful character when compared with most other scriptures. The final text of the Qur'an was completed prior to Muhammad's death (632 C.E.).

To Muslims, the Qur'an is without question the Word of God. The word *qur'an* means "to be recited." Though the Hebrew Bible and Christian New Testament are considered to be holy books, the Qur'an supersedes these as the final authority. It was written in Arabic—a Semitic language like Hebrew. According to traditionalist Muslims, the Qur'an is not translatable, since it was revealed to Muhammad in Arabic. For instance, an English version of the Qur'an is simply not the Qur'an. It is interesting to note the numerous references the Qur'an makes to Jewish as well as Christian subjects. Does the following story sound familiar?

> "And when they presented themselves before Joseph, they said: 'Noble prince, we and our people are scourged with famine. We have brought but little money. Give us some corn, and be charitable to us: Allah rewards the charitable.'

'Do you know,' he replied, 'what you
did to Joseph and his brother in your
ignorance?'

They cried: 'Can you indeed be Joseph?'

'I am Joseph,' he answered, 'and this is my
brother. Allah has been gracious to us. Those
that keep from evil and endure with fortitude,
Allah will not deny them their reward.'"[14]

Your Bible awaits you. Pull it out and read Chapters 44 and
45 of the book of Genesis. If you can obtain a copy of the
Qur'an, you will find the entire story of Joseph in the twelfth
chapter. It is fascinating reading. You can decide which version
you like best.

Judaism

From the Hebrew Bible, one of the Enthronement Hymns:

"Make a joyful shout to the Lord, all you lands!
Serve the Lord with gladness;
Come before His presence with singing.
Know that the Lord, He *is* God;
It is He *who* has made us, and not we
    ourselves;
We are His people and the sheep of His
    pasture.
Enter into His gates with thanksgiving,
And into His courts with praise.
Be thankful to Him, *and* bless His name.
For the Lord *is* good;
His mercy *is* everlasting,
And His truth *endures* to all generations."[15]

Christianity

From the New Testament, the words of Jesus from the Sermon on the Mount:

> "Blessed *are* the poor in spirit,
>   For theirs is the kingdom of heaven.
> Blessed *are* those who mourn,
>   For they shall be comforted.
> Blessed *are* the meek,
>   For they shall inherit the earth.
> Blessed *are* those who hunger and thirst for
>   righteousness,
>   For they shall be filled.
> Blessed *are* the merciful,
>   For they shall obtain mercy.
> Blessed *are* the pure in heart,
>   For they shall see God.
> Blessed *are* the peacemakers,
>   For they shall be called sons of God.
> Blessed *are* those who are persecuted for
>   righteousness' sake,
>   For theirs is the kingdom of heaven."[16]

Inclusion of the Bible in this list is to help you see that it is but one of many sacred writings.

American Civil Religion

What do we mean by "American Civil Religion"? After all, isn't the government supposed to stay out of religious matters? Well, have you ever attended the annual ritual festival commemorating our nation's deliverance from the hands of the tyrannical British King George? It sounds kind of funny to describe the Fourth of July holiday in such Mosaic terms, but in a way it makes some sense. Have you ever considered that the United States of America has its holy scriptures?[17] The Declaration of Independence and the Constitution comprise the scriptures of American civil religion. Take a look at these familiar words of the Declaration of Independence:

> We hold these truths to be self-evident, that all men are created equal, that they are endowed by their Creator with certain unalienable Rights, that among these are Life, Liberty, and the pursuit of Happiness.[18]

These words sound pretty religious to me. Perhaps they do to you too. If Confucius could write about governmental prin-

"A new heart I will give you, and a new spirit I will put within you."
—Ezekiel 36:26

ciples in spiritual context, then why couldn't Thomas Jefferson and company do the same? Just because our government does not promote any one religion over another does not mean that people who comprise the government are void of spirituality. Certainly the *scriptures* of American Civil Religion have a certain spiritual element to them.

Mormonism

While we are on the subject of America and religion, let us visit one of the fastest-growing religious movements, The Church of Jesus Christ of Latter-day Saints, or "the Mormons." What is unique about the Mormons when compared with other denominations is that they have their own scriptures, *The Book of Mormon.*

According to their tradition, in 1823 Joseph Smith of New York State received a vision of an angel, Moroni, who directed him to some ancient gold plates buried in the ground near his home. Moroni instructed him that at the right time he would be able to translate these plates. In 1830 The Book of Mormon was first published. It consists of fifteen different books and presumably covers the period of time from 600 B.C.E. to 421 C.E. Here is a short sample from The Book of Mormon:

> "And whatsoever ye shall ask the Father
> in my name, which is right, believing
> that ye shall receive, behold it shall be
> given unto you."[19]

Again, another scripture that reads amazingly like the Bible. Look up Matthew 21:22, Mark 11:24, John 11:22—14:13.

Christian Science

Another indigenous American denomination is Christian Science. Founded in Boston by Mary Baker Eddy in 1881, Christian Science became the first metaphysically based Christian religious movement in America. In 1875 Eddy published *Science and Health With Key to the Scriptures,* a book that has become almost like scripture to Christian Science followers over the years. Interestingly, the book is organized with verse numbers like many scriptures. Here is Chapter IV, "Christian Science Versus Spiritualism," verses 1–11, from the Authorized Version of *Science and Health:*

> Mortal existence is an enigma. Every day is a mystery. The testimony of the corporeal senses cannot inform us what is real and what is delusive, but the revelations of Christian Science unlock the treasures of Truth. Whatever is false or sinful can never enter the atmosphere of Spirit. There is but one Spirit. Man is never God, but spiritual man, made in God's like-

ness, reflects God. In this scientific reflection the Ego and the Father are inseparable. The supposition that corporeal beings are spirits, or that there are good and evil spirits, is a mistake.[20]

Perhaps you noticed Mary Baker Eddy's subtle reference to the Bible in this paragraph. Look up Genesis 1:26–27.

Unity

If the Mormons and Christian Scientists have scriptures, then why not Unity? Let us look at their similarities. All are offshoots of mainstream Christianity. All are indigenous American religious movements. All honor the Bible, but have their own slant on interpreting it. Mormon spirituality is expressed in its scripture, The Book of Mormon, Christian Science through *Science and Health.* What do you think about naming *Lessons in Truth* as the first Unity scripture? Wasn't *Lessons in Truth* revealed through Emilie Cady?

Most metaphysical Christians might find this line of reasoning preposterous. However, if you think about it, *Lessons in Truth* has almost become a scripture within Unity. I recall having to memorize the four denials and affirmations from *Lessons in Truth* during my ministerial school training. If we were to construct a canon of Unity scripture, it might include such writings as: *Lessons in Truth, Christian Healing, What Are You?* and so forth. These are the recommended study books for those wishing to enter training as a Unity teacher or minister. Possibly *The Quest* will gain this status at a future date. Perhaps we don't hold these Unity scriptures in as high esteem as the Bible, but we sure seem to read them more. About those denials and affirmations:

First: There is no evil. . . .

Second: There is no absence of life, substance, or intelligence anywhere. . . .

Third: Pain, sickness, poverty, old age, and death cannot master me, for they are not real.

Fourth: There is nothing in all the universe for me to fear, for greater is He that is within me than he that is in the world. . . .[21]

First: *God is life, love, intelligence, substance, omnipotence, omniscience, omnipresence. . . .*

Second: *I am a child or manifestation of God, and every moment His life, love, wisdom, power flow into and through me. I am one with God and am governed by His law. . . .*

Third: *I am Spirit, perfect, holy, harmonious. Nothing can hurt me or make me sick or afraid, for Spirit is God, and God cannot be sick or hurt or afraid. I manifest my real Self through this body now.*

Fourth: *God works in me to will and to do whatsoever He wishes me to do, and He cannot fail. . . .*[22]

Summary

It is my sincere hope that this journey through some of the world's scriptures has been eye-opening, and *Bible Opening*. We can readily see that the Bible is but one of numerous other scriptures, each influencing the other, each borrowing from the other, each possessing universal principles of Truth, each sacred to its followers. The old saying *there is nothing new under the sun* definitely applies to the study of scripture, a practice which blesses and uplifts us through the power of the Word.

Notes

1. Taken from the Greek word *kanon* meaning "rod, rule or cane," *canon* refer to those writings recognized as authoritative, and which are, therefore, included in the Bible.

2. Passover is also known as the feast of unleavened bread.

3. The traditional Christmas story is actually a blending of two stories found in Matthew 1:18—2:23 and Luke 1:26—2:20. Discrepancies between the accounts are ignored in order to create a smooth-flowing narrative.

4. From *The Upanishads,* Volume IV, as translated into English by Swami Nikhilananda and published by the Ramakrishna-Vivekananda Center of New York, copyright 1959 by Swami Nikhilananda.

5. *The Bhagavad Gita,* as translated into English by Swami Nikhilananda, published by the Ramakrishna-Vivekananda Center of New York, copyright 1944 by Swami Nikhilananda.

6. Enlightened, possessing divine wisdom. The title was applied to Siddhartha Gautama, acknowledging his unique status as an enlightened master.

7. Proverbs 23:7, KJV.

8. P. Lal (trans.), *The Dhammapada* (New York: Farrar, Straus & Giroux, 1967), p. 39.

9. Gia-fu Feng and Jane English (trans.), *Tao Te Ching* (New York: Vintage Books, 1972), p. 29.

10. Lionel Giles (trans.), *The Analects of Confucius* (New York: The Heritage Press, 1970), pp. 22–24.

11. Modern-day Iran.

12. Robert O. Ballou (ed.), *The Portable World Bible* (New York: Penguin Books, 1976), p. 173.

13. Matthew 2:1.

14. N. J. Dawood (trans.), *The Koran* (Middlesex: Penguin Classics 1956, Fourth revised edition 1974), copyright © N. J. Dawood, 1956, 1959, 1966, 1968, 1974, pp. 45–46. Reproduced by permission of Penguin Books Ltd.

15. Psalm 100:1–5, NKJV.

16. Matthew 5:3–10, NKJV.

17. Certainly not all readers of this book are United States citizens. Civil religion and its corresponding scriptures exist in all nations of the world.

18. From the second paragraph of the *Declaration of Independence.*

19. 3 Nephi 18:20, Joseph Smith, Jun. (trans.), *The Book of Mormon* (Salt Lake City: The Church of Jesus Christ of Latter-day Saints, 1981), p. 443.

20. Mary Baker Eddy, *Science and Health With Key to the Scriptures,* Boston: Trustees under the Will of Mary Baker G. Eddy, 1934), p. 70.

21. H. Emilie Cady, *Lessons in Truth* (Unity Village: Unity Books, 1995) pp. 51–52.

22. Ibid., pp. 62–64.

Chapter 4

Metaphysical Christianity's Biblical Heritage

This book has addressed the lack of biblical knowledge among people, especially metaphysical Christians. From this premise, I have demonstrated that this condition is due in part to the unconventional nature of the Bible's literary formation. However, there is another major factor to consider, one which was only touched upon in Chapter 1, that of changes in our modern society.

A hundred years ago there was no radio[1] or television. Books, newspapers, and the sound of the wind in the trees were the external stimuli of the day. Most homes did not have telephones or electric lights. People read books. People read their Bibles. People discussed their reading with each other. Literary societies were common. The written word was God.

Our "God" has changed. Today's information age and its warp speed has firmly taken hold. We are now constantly bombarded with media, often filling our eyes and ears to capacity. Our civilization has embraced a new "God," the video screen. Whether our choice is cable TV, video games, or the computer monitor, we have become a video culture. We play, shop, baby-sit our children, acquire news, entertain ourselves, and even write—all in front of a video screen.[2] The video medium with its visual images and mechanically reproduced sounds now reigns supreme.

On the other hand, the world of books is a world of words. Though some books have illustrations, words are their primary force. The information age has pushed the written word into the backseat behind the almighty boob tube. While we can almost instantly assimilate the moving pictures and audible sounds of television into our psychological bloodstream, books and their printed words require much more time to read and absorb. Because of their ease of use, graphics-oriented displays[3] have replaced word commands in today's personal computers. It's no wonder that the video screen has surpassed the written word as the choice of most modern people.

"Do not fear, greatly beloved, you are safe. Be strong and courageous!"
—Daniel 10:19

I do not wish to imply that books and reading are passé— quite the contrary. There are more books, newspapers, and periodicals being published than ever before. However, today's publications, unless they are strictly words, are embellished with many more graphic images than they once were. Have you ever leafed through a book or magazine just to scan the pictures? Pick up a book or newspaper from the past century and, except for the occasional line drawing, you'll be hard pressed to find many pictures. Yet even with the proliferation of and improvements in books and other reading material, we do not read nearly as much as we did in the past.

When we do read, our choices are nearly inexhaustible. A simple walk through your local supermarket will assault your senses with a plethora of reading options. The checkout stand alone is a veritable literary delicatessen, though much of its fare may cause cerebral indigestion. When we read books, we often pick ones by popular authors such as Tom Clancy, Danielle Steele, or Michael Crichton, and the like. These authors grab us. Their use of words paints vivid images, evokes strong feelings, and reveals concepts in a manner that is both clever and convincing. As a result, their books sell like hotcakes.

Your friend asks you, "Read any good books lately?" You say, "Oh, I'm reading the latest book by (famous author)." And your friend responds, "May I borrow it when you're done?" This conversation seldom occurs when the Bible is the book in question. Can you imagine this discussion? Friend: "Read any good books lately?" You: "Oh yeah, this New Revised Standard Version of Leviticus is just riveting." Friend: "Oh really, can I see it too?" Sounds pretty laughable, doesn't it?

Although the Bible may be at the top of the best-seller list, it is not at the top of the most-often-read list. Made-for-TV movies about the Bible are often the only contacts some people have with Bible stories and characters. The overall societal impetus for reading the Bible is not especially strong. In stricter religious circles, people are simply scared into reading the Bible, impelled by fear rather than earnest desire. Others, motivated by duty, are obliged

"As you have done, it shall be done to you."
—Obadiah 1:15

to study the Bible in order to fulfill some special academic requirement. And, there are a handful who love the Bible and read it with great enthusiasm and intelligence. The rest of us are busy watching television, going to movies, playing with our computers and, occasionally, reading books. The Bible is usually not the book sitting on our nightstand awaiting our eager eyes.

Metaphysical Christianity and the Bible

My purpose in discussing these societal changes has a great deal to do with the subject of this chapter. Inherent in the words *metaphysical Christianity* is an expectation of biblical relationship. Metaphysical Christianity would not be Christian without it. Our knowledge about the life and teachings of Jesus Christ is found primarily in the Bible. The chief contributors to metaphysical Christianity's biblical heritage knew this and spent much of their time studying the Bible. However, these people, for the most part, lived in the world of books and not the video screen. Generally speaking, they were not members of our most recent generation of ministers and teachers. This circumstance has had an adverse impact upon the biblical aptitude of most metaphysical Christians.

For example, the vast majority of metaphysical Christian churches do not conduct Bible study classes. If they do, these classes are almost always infrequently held and sparsely attended. Because of this, most metaphysical Christians today are ignorant of their rich biblical heritage and, therefore, rarely avail themselves of it in their spiritual quest.

Also, metaphysical Christians often refer to the Bible as a spiritual handbook or textbook. Yet how many of these people actually use the Bible as a handbook for daily living? Very few. If this were the case, they would all be going to church with Bibles in hand[4] or there would be Bibles in the pews as in more traditional churches.

Some conservative Christian denominations accuse metaphysical Christianity of not being Christian or Bible-based.[5] Is this an erroneous label or an honest appraisal? On the basis of current practice, they may have a point. Maybe it doesn't matter to the average Unity or Religious Science churchgoer, but perhaps it is time that it does matter.

Metaphysical Christianity has an extensive biblical heritage and fills a distinctive niche in the overall world of the Bible. Decided differences exist between the metaphysical Christian and the more traditional Christian approach to the Bible. Central to these differences is how each group views the Bible's words. Traditional Christianity sees the Bible as the Absolute Word of God. The metaphysician acknowledges the Bible as inspired writing in which universal Truths are expressed.

To illustrate: Have you ever watched a football game on TV and noticed someone in the stands holding up a banner that read **John 3:16**? Did you look up John 3:16 in your Bible? I'll bet you didn't. Allow me to do it for you this time:

> "For God so loved the world that He gave His only begotten Son, that whoever believes in Him should not perish but have everlasting life."[6]

This passage often evokes a strong emotional response from traditional Christians. It is perhaps the most often quoted scripture by those seeking to convert others to Christianity. The centerpiece of this passage is the phrase "only begotten Son."

The question arises, Was Jesus referring to himself in this verse? On the surface, John 3:16 implies that everlasting life is only attainable through a faith in Jesus Christ.

According to metaphysical Christianity, "the only begotten Son" does not exclusively refer to Jesus, but to the Christ or divine Spirit in everyone. This Christ was present in Jesus as much as it is in every other person. If we believe in the power of the Christ to help us, and we feel that presence within, we can experience everlasting life and other spiritual blessings. What sets Jesus apart from the bulk of humanity is that he better demonstrated this spiritual potential in his life. Pick any of the four Gospels and read about his miracles. You'll see what I mean.

> **"These are the things that you shall do: Speak the truth to one another, render in your gates judgments that are true and make for peace."**
> —Zechariah 8:16

Metaphysical Christianity offers an approach to Bible interpretation that speaks to the heart of the Truth seeker. The question is always, How does this Bible story or passage apply to practical everyday life? The problem for metaphysical Christianity in advancing its particular biblical perspective lies in the very word *heritage*. Let us now examine this heritage in the hope of instilling a desire to explore the Bible and its spiritual treasure. Who were these "Bible thumpers" of the past?

Charles Fillmore

Unity's biblical heritage begins with its co-founder Charles Fillmore. An avid Bible student, he authored *Mysteries of Genesis* and *Mysteries of John*, two books devoted entirely to the interpretation of these notable biblical books. Here are selections from each:

From *Mysteries of Genesis,* Charles Fillmore interprets the inner struggle Jacob experienced wrestling with the angel (Genesis 32:3–28):

> Until love has done its perfect work man is fearful. Jacob feared to meet Esau. We find it hard to face the full claims of the body (Esau) after we have cheated it of its birthright, unity of soul and body in spiritual thought. Divine courage must supplant this fear before we are equal to facing the consequences of our self-centered thoughts and to taking up the task of harmonizing all our forces. But the vital power of Spirit animates the body, and it responds readily to our true thought when we give it of our substance.[7]

From *Mysteries of John,* Charles Fillmore comments on the raising of Lazarus by Jesus (John 11:17–44):

> We should ever remember that the youth we love so well never dies; it is merely asleep in the subconscious—Jesus said that Lazarus was not dead. People grow old because they let the youth idea fall asleep. This idea is not dead but is sleeping, and the understanding I AM (Jesus) goes to awaken it. . . .

Eternal youth is one of these God-given ideas that
man loves. Jesus loved Lazarus.[8]

Charles Fillmore was also the primary author of Unity's
Metaphysical Bible Dictionary. Contained within the more than
700 pages of this book are definitions for every person and
place mentioned in the Bible and its metaphysical interpretation. It is an awesome piece of work and required many years
to complete. Read by people throughout the metaphysical
Christian world, there is nothing else like it. The *Metaphysical
Bible Dictionary* stands alone as the standard and is a must for
any serious Bible student. Here is a small sample:

> **Rebekah,** re-bek'-ah (Heb.)—*tying firmly; fastening;
> binding; noosed cord; captivating; snare; beauty that
> ensnares; grace that enraptures.*
>   Daughter of Bethuel, wife of Isaac, and mother
> of Jacob and Esau (Gen. 24:15–67). The name is
> spelled "Rebecca" in Romans 9:10.
> **Meta**—The soul's natural delight in beauty. This
> essence of the soul is continually going forth and
> making attachments with the harmonious and
> beautiful (interpretation of Gen. 24:59).[9]

To have written such an extensive Bible book undoubtedly
places Charles Fillmore in the class of *Bible thumper par excellence.* His book *The Revealing Word,* a glossary of spiritual
terminology, is also helpful.

Elizabeth Sand Turner

Where Charles Fillmore ends, Elizabeth Sand Turner begins. Her books are condensed narratives of significant Bible
stories arranged in chronological order along with their corresponding metaphysical interpretations. Throughout her books,

she often refers to Charles Fillmore's writings, especially the *Metaphysical Bible Dictionary,* to support her ideas. She wrote three volumes: *Let There Be Light* (Old Testament), *Your Hope of Glory* (New Testament—Gospels), *Be Ye Transformed* (New Testament—Acts, Epistles, Revelation). Make sure these three books are in your Bible study library.

In this excerpt from *Be Ye Transformed,* she describes Paul's speech to the Athenians at the Areopagus (Acts 17:15–34):

> In contrast to his usual direct manner of presenting Christ as the Savior, Paul began by complimenting the Athenians on their interest in religion and pointed to the altar that had been inscribed "to an unknown god" (Acts 17:23). This god was the God of the universe, Paul said, who is spiritual in nature and "does not live in shrines made by human hands" (Acts 17:24). God is the Father of all men and they should seek Him "in the hope that they might feel after him and find him. Yet he is not far from each one of us, for "In him we live and move and have our being." (Acts 17:27, 28 RSV). God, he continued, does not condemn men for idolatry when they are ignorant but now He requires that they repent, for He will judge the world in righteousness by "a man whom he has appointed" and whom He raised from the dead, Jesus Christ.
>
> The idea of resurrection was met with ridicule by the majority of Paul's hearers. Though a few were impressed, the Christ message did not gain a foothold in Athens during Paul's lifetime.[10]

She follows this narration with an interpretation (note the reference to the *Metaphysical Bible Dictionary*):

> To all appearances this was a defeat for Paul, and the reason lies in a spiritual interpretation of the

incident. "Athens stands for the intellectual center in man" (MD p. 78). The intellect can be the forerunner of spiritual illumination but when it is given wholly to mental interests, as in the case of the Athenians, it presents a closed door to Truth. It is wise to refrain from further attempts to influence such a mind.[11]

Other Unity Writers

Throughout the years a number of other Unity ministers have contributed books on Bible interpretation. In this section, I have included a brief description of some of their books along with excerpts from each. Here is an alphabetical listing according to last name:

Eric Butterworth—*Discover the Power Within You* guides the reader through the essential teachings of Jesus as revealed in the four Gospels and especially the Sermon on the Mount. In this example, Eric Butterworth interprets Jesus' warning about casting "pearls before swine" (Mt. 7:6):

> The word "cynic" comes from the Greek word that means *dog*. We can see that Jesus is again using a classic figure of speech. He is not calling narrow people swine or canines. He is simply saying, "Don't waste your time trying to present the Truth to the cynical person. He won't understand it and he will only tear your arguments to pieces."[12]

William Cameron—*Great Dramas of the Bible* presents spiritual ideas through twenty-six Bible stories. William Cameron delightfully weaves Bible scholarship, metaphysical interpretation, and humor into the book. Here is his preamble to the story of Jonah:

Now, the mention of Jonah or any fish story can bring a smile. It is well known that most fishermen catch their best fish by the "tale" and that there is a miracle of sorts involved in all fish stories—nothing grows quite so fast as a fish from the time it bites until it gets away!

The big news in the story of Jonah is that it is the man who gets away from the fish, and for many people that has been hard to swallow. Maybe we can get past the question of credibility with this story: A man said to a fisherman, "I notice that in telling about the fish you caught, you vary the size with different listeners." "Yes," answered the fisherman. "I never tell a man more than I think he'll believe."[13]

Hypatia Hasbrouck—*The Trip to Bethlehem* is exactly what it is subtitled, *The Traditional Christmas Story as a Guide to Spiritual Transformation*. This book is a well-written metaphysical interpretation of the elements of the Christmas story and invites readers to relate the story to their own inner, psychological processes. The book also contains interpretations of non-biblical elements of the Christmas story as well. Consider Hypatia Hasbrouck's interpretation of Bethlehem:

Regardless of where Jesus was actually born, metaphysically speaking, the trip to Bethlehem is essential, not simply to fulfill the prophecy, but because of the meaning of the name, the location and character of the city, and its connection with David. Bethlehem literally means house of bread or food, house of sustenance, house of living. Metaphysically, the city represents a consciousness of omnipresent substance or divine energy which provides everything needed to create and sustain everything, including the emerging Christ.[14]

Charles Neal—*Revelation: The Road to Overcoming* is an interpretation of the book of Revelation. Charles Neal intelligently unveils the mysterious symbology of this challenging biblical book in a down-to-earth, practical manner. Here is his interpretation of the great earthquake described in Revelation 6:12–17—7:1–17:

> The image of the earthquake is an excellent one. Who in life has not suffered some earthshaking experience, when the ground on which we stood seemed to tremble, and the house of life that we had so painstakingly built came crashing to the ground? The death of a loved one, a grievous financial loss, a disabling accident, a serious illness, the loss of employment, a brush with the law, a beloved child running away from home—the list of possibilities is endless. Any of these and other misfortunes can leave us shaken, bewildered, uncertain. The sun of life is blotted out. God has seemingly forsaken us. What can we now believe in? Where can we safely stand? Such are the reactions of all who are without spiritual resources.[15]

J. Sig Paulson/Ric Dickerson—*Revelation: The Book of Unity* is another book that delves into the book of Revelation. However, unlike the previous book, this one is a dialogue between Sig Paulson, a Unity minister, and Ric Dickerson, a teacher of neuroscience. We pick up the conversation in the opening chapter:

> *Paulson* . . . Thus we know that this is the revelation from Jesus Christ as it was revealed to the servant John. The revelation is not John's; he was just the messenger who delivered it. The revelation has been described in a number of ways, and perhaps

the most significant one is this: *the kingdom of God is within you.*

It seems quite likely that the person who wrote this book is not the disciple John. But we need not be concerned about that here. For our purpose, we can think of John as representing love. This is the revelation that comes through the activity of love. We are blessed and happy as we receive the prophecy, and we are prepared at this time to understand the message of the revelation.

Dickerson . . . I would like to speak about this from a little different angle, from a scientific point of view. Many years ago, Einstein described the field of revelation, this underlying field of existence we talk about in our Unity affirmations. We call it the Power and the Presence, the omnipresence of God. He described it as a unified field of energy underlying and supporting all of creation. . . .

Paulson . . . We might say that the revelation comes through Einstein as the unified-field-of-energy theory, and through Jesus Christ as "the fields . . . already white for harvest."[16]

Catherine Ponder—*The Millionaire From Nazareth* is but one among several books Catherine Ponder has written about the Bible. All of her books draw forth teachings of prosperity from scripture. In this selection, she comments on the story of the widow's mite, found in Mark 12:41–44 and Luke 21:1–4:

Most of us get into a "widow state of mind" at some point in our lives. Many of us are still trying to rise out of that belief in lack which the widow symbolized: (1) a feeling of being separated from our good, or (2) a feeling of being without worldly protection and power.

When you feel that you are in a state of lack and separated from your good, like this widow you need to do something drastic—first in your thinking, then in your actions—in order to rise out of that state of limitation.[17]

Georgiana Tree West—*Prosperity's Ten Commandments* is a book much in the same vein as Catherine Ponder's in that prosperity is the main focus. Georgiana Tree West puts an unorthodox but effective spin on the Ten Commandments received by Moses. The eighth commandment ordinarily reads: "You shall not steal" (Ex. 20:15). Georgiana Tree West interprets it this way:

> You shall not seek something for nothing. . . .
>
> The eighth commandment, like all the others, covers a broad field of human activities. Its meaning can by no means be confined to the mere act of committing petty or grand larceny. To *steal,* according to Webster, means "to take . . . without right or leave and with intent to keep . . . wrongfully." Many self-righteous people believe that if they do not gain possession of another's property unlawfully they are not disobeying the eighth commandment. They condemn the misguided burglar, pickpocket, or embezzler, and as a rule are most insistent that these criminals be severely punished. This sharp intolerance of the weaknesses of others is characteristic of those who keep the letter of the law but violate its spirit.[18]

Ernest C. Wilson—*The Week That Changed the World* focuses on the final week of Jesus' life. Ernest Wilson skillfully pulls together scripture, biblical speculation, and metaphysical interpretation into a narrative that is very readable. In the chapter "Peter, the Impetuous," he interprets Peter's denial of Jesus before the cock crowed:

> How much of Peter there is in all of us! We want to be strong, faithful to the Truth we know. When by thought or word or act we fail to measure up to what we know in theory, our chagrin is great. We go over and over in thought what we might have said or done, how we might have presented ourself better. We like to think that we will never make the same mistake again, and are impatient because often our progress seems so much slower than we could wish.[19]

Other Metaphysical Christian Writings

The body of Bible interpretation writings is certainly not limited to these eight Unity authors. Unity School of Christianity has published thousands of books and periodicals over the past hundred years, most of which have biblical material. Those you might consider investigating include *Old Weekly Unity* (now out of print), *Unity Magazine*, and the Old Testament and New Testament Bible study syllabuses. Additionally, Charles Fillmore, H. Emilie Cady, and Eric Butterworth[20] use the Bible extensively in all of their books.

Emmet Fox

Among non-Unity writers and contributors to metaphysical Christianity's biblical heritage, Emmet Fox stands out above the crowd. His book *The Sermon on the Mount* is one of the best-selling books, let alone Bible books, in metaphysical Christendom. He has also authored a companion volume, *The Ten Commandments*. Both books bring a practical, metaphysical perspective to the scriptures they cover.

From *The Sermon on the Mount,* Emmet Fox explains Matthew 5:13–16:

> In this wonderful passage Jesus is addressing those who have awakened to the understanding of material bondage, and have acquired some spiritual understanding of the nature of Being. That is to say, he is addressing those who understand the meaning of the Allness of God or Good, and the powerlessness of evil in the face of Truth. Such people he describes as being *the salt of the earth,* and *the light of the world;* and, indeed, that is not too much to claim for those who understand the Truth, and who *really live the life that corresponds to it.* It is possible, and, in fact, only too easy, to accept these vital principles as being true; to love the beauty in them; and yet not to put them consistently into practice in one's own life; but this is a perilous attitude, for in that case *the salt has lost its savour,* and is good for nothing but to be cast out and trodden under foot.[21]

George Lamsa

During the 1960s a scholar by the name of George Lamsa came to Unity School of Christianity. He significantly influenced the biblical thinking of many ministers and teachers who came in contact with him and his ideas. He is the author of numerous Bible study books. A native of present-day Iraq, George Lamsa contributed a uniquely Middle Eastern perspective to biblical study. His protégés, Dr. Rocco Errico and Dr. Paul C. Barrett, continue to further his work. However, George Lamsa is best known for his controversial English translation of the Bible (to be reviewed in Chapter 5, "Getting Started").

Metaphysical Bible Teachers

Any discussion of Unity's biblical heritage must include not only prominent writers but also teachers. Though these people have not published books on Bible interpretation, they have made their mark in the classroom at Unity School of Christianity and in field ministry. I have made every effort to compile a comprehensive list. In approximate chronological order, they are Francis Gable, Herbert Hunt, Ed Rabel, Frank Giudici, Paul Barrett, Wayne Manning, Sallye Taylor, and the current chairperson of Biblical Studies, Laura Barrett.

Furthermore, the larger field of New Thought[22] has also used the Bible as a teaching source. Phineas P. Quimby, usually considered the founder of New Thought, showed great familiarity with the Bible. Mary Baker Eddy's one-time follower, Emma Curtis Hopkins, also greatly stressed the Bible and majorly influenced Cady and the Fillmores. Hopkins' emphasis on scripture also impacted Annie Rix Militz, one of New Thought's most important leaders, as well as Ernest Holmes, the founder of Religious Science and *Science of Mind* magazine which has had a large influence in the metaphysical community. Bible study was also central to Malinda Cramer, the co-founder of Divine Science.

Summary

We can plainly see that metaphysical Christianity has a considerable biblical heritage. From Charles Fillmore to Emmet Fox, each of these writers has provided some exceptional books on Bible interpretation. However, in order to truly appreciate their efforts, we must pry ourselves away from our video screens long enough to open our Bibles.

Now that you are ready to study the Bible for yourself, how do you begin? Part II of this book will assist you in assembling the tools you'll need to succeed at Bible study. Why not get started today? (There's probably not much worth watching on TV tonight anyhow!)

Notes

1. In 1895 the first radio signals were transmitted by the Italian engineer, Guglielmo Marconi.

2. This book was written using an NEC Powermate 386/20 personal computer and an IBM 8512 VGA monitor.

3. Apple's Macintosh and Microsoft's Windows environments are prime examples.

4. In fourteen years of field ministry, I have witnessed only a few people who regularly bring their Bibles to church.

5. Refer to *Kingdom of the Cults* by Walter Martin and *Encyclopedic Handbook of Cults in America,* by J. Gordon Melton. These books are available in your local library or Christian bookstore.

6. John 3:16, NKJV.

7. Charles Fillmore, *Mysteries of Genesis* (Unity Village: Unity School of Christianity, 1989), pp. 257–58.

8. Charles Fillmore, *Mysteries of John* (Unity Village: Unity Books, 1997), p. 110.

9. *Metaphysical Bible Dictionary* (Unity Village: Unity Books, 1995), p. 547.

10. Elizabeth Sand Turner, *Be Ye Transformed* (Unity Village: Unity Books, 1996), pp. 83–84.

11. Ibid., p. 84.

12. Eric Butterworth, *Discover the Power Within You* (New York: HarperCollins, 1968), p. 140.

13. William Earle Cameron, *Great Dramas of the Bible* (Unity Village: Unity School of Christianity, 1984), p. 53.

14. Hypatia Hasbrouck, *The Trip to Bethlehem* (Seattle: Peanut Butter Publishing, 1995), p. 37, available from the author at 234 W. Fairfield St., Gladstone, OR 97027-2027.

15. Charles A. Neal, *Revelation: The Road to Overcoming* (Unity Village: Unity School of Christianity, 1990), pp. 107–08.

16. J. Sig Paulson & Ric Dickerson, *Revelation: The Book of Unity* (Unity Village: Unity School of Christianity, 1981), pp. 6–9.

17. Used by permission of the author, copyright 1979, Catherine Ponder, P.O. Drawer 1278, Palm Desert, California, 92261. Publishers: DeVorss & Co., Marina del Rey, CA 90294.

18. Georgiana Tree West, *Prosperity's Ten Commandments* (Unity Village: Unity Books, 1996), p. 101.

19. Ernest C. Wilson, *The Week That Changed the World* (Unity Village: Unity School of Christianity, 1990), p. 140.

20. Eric Butterworth's *Metamorality,* published by Unity School of Christianity, is a fresh interpretation of the Ten Commandments. It was formerly published by Harper & Row under the name *How to Break the Ten Commandments.*

21. Emmet Fox, *The Sermon on the Mount* (New York: HarperCollins, 1938), pp. 50–51.

22. The traditional name for the American religious movement that, loosely speaking, includes Unity, Religious Science, and Divine Science as well as others. New Thought and Christian Science are also similar. In this book, I've called this *metaphysical Christianity.*

Part II.

Assembling the Tools of Bible Study

Chapter 5

Getting Started

Congratulations! You've made it to Part II, Assembling the Tools of Bible Study. By now you've decided that the Bible might be worth studying. It truly is. These next three chapters will explain to you what resources are available in successfully studying the Bible. Taking our cue from the title of this chapter, let's get started.

Your exploration of the Bible begins by selecting a good translation. It's a lot like the "wise man who built his house on rock" rather than the "foolish man who built his house on sand."[1] The translation you select is the foundation upon which you will build your interpretations. In a way, choosing a translation is the first step in the interpretation process. Your assignment is to find a Bible that serves your needs as a student and has words that speak to your soul. Some Bibles may click with you, others may not. No one version is better than another, although some may be more accurate translations than others. You may wonder how English translations of the Bible came to be. Read on.

English Bible Translation

Along with being history's most popular book, the Bible is also its most translated. As we have already learned, the

Bible was written in ancient languages by many different people over hundreds of years. Without an English translation, 99.9 percent of us would be unable to read the Bible. What if there were no translations? Can you imagine what it would be like to read the ancient manuscripts? Try your hand at reading this:

מזמור לדוד יהוה רצי לא אחסר

How is your Hebrew these days? The text reads backwards, from right to left. You may have recognized the word for *Lord,* יהוה, which transliterates as YHWH. Hebrew was originally written with only consonants, as displayed here. The King James Version of this well-known verse reads, "The Lord is my shepherd; I shall not want" (Ps. 23:1).

ΠΑΤΕΡ ΗΜΩΝ Ο ΕΝ ΤΟΙΣ ΟΥΡΑΝΟΙΣ

ΑΓΙΑΣΘΗΤΩ ΤΟ ΟΝΟΜΑ ΣΟΥ

ΕΛΘΕΤΩ Η ΒΑΣΙΛΕΙΑ ΣΟΥ

ΓΕΝΗΘΗΤΩ ΤΟ ΘΕΛΗΜΑ ΣΟΥ

ΩΣ ΕΝ ΟΥΡΑΝΩ ΚΑΙ ΕΠΙ ΓΗΣ

ΤΟΝ ΑΡΤΟΝ ΗΜΩΝ ΤΟΝ ΕΠΙΟΥΣΙΟΝ ΔΟΣ ΗΜΙΝ ΣΗΜΕΡΟΝ

ΚΑΙ ΑΦΕΣ ΗΜΙΝ ΤΑ ΟΦΕΙΛΗΜΑΤΑ ΗΜΩΝ

ΩΣ ΚΑΙ ΗΜΕΙΣ ΑΦΗΚΑΜΕΝ ΤΟΙΣ ΟΦΕΙΛΕΙΤΑΙΣ ΗΜΩΝ

ΚΑΙ ΜΗ ΕΙΣΕΝΕΓΚΗΣ ΗΜΑΣ ΕΙΣ ΠΕΙΡΑΣΜΟΝ

ΑΛΛΑ ΡΥΣΑΙ ΗΜΑΣ ΑΠΟ ΤΟΥ ΠΟΝΗΡΟΥ

After trying to read the previous paragraph, you might be saying to yourself, "It's all Greek to me!" This passage may remind you more of a drive through a college neighborhood than the Lord's Prayer. The words above are written in all uppercase Greek letters as they might have appeared in an early manuscript. Were you able to recognize any words? The first one, ΠΑΤΕΡ, phonetically becomes PATER, meaning "father." Most of us would prefer to read this passage in good old basic English than Greek.

Thankfully, over the past 600 years, practically hundreds of English translations have been published. Several were already in existence prior to the famous King James Version of 1611. English translations of various biblical books appeared as early as the eighth century C.E. Try your hand at reading the Lord's Prayer in the Anglo-Saxon of that age:

> Uren Fader dhic art in heofnas
> Sic gehalyed dhin noma
> To cymedh dhin ric
> Sic dhin willa sue is in heofnas and in eardhs
> Vren hlaf ofer wirthe sel us to daeg
> And forgef us scylda urna
> Sue we forgefan sculdgun vrum
> And no inleadh vridk in costung
> Als gefrig vrich fro ifle[2]

Unless you are an English-language specialist, the Anglo-Saxon Lord's Prayer may have been a bit perplexing to read. Here are a few words you may have been able to pick out: *Fader* = Father, *heofnas* = heaven, *gehalyed* = hallowed, *willa* = will, *eardhs* = earth, *forgef* = forgive, *ifle* = evil. Anglo-Saxon was the language of the Germanic peoples who invaded England during the fifth century C.E. and is the root of our modern English language.

The first complete translation of the Bible into English was accomplished in 1382 and is attributed to the scholar and reformer John Wycliffe. The English language had undergone significant changes since the Norman conquest of England in 1066. Latin had entered Anglo-Saxon via the French of the Normans and had blended together into a distinct English tongue. This version of the Bible, based on the Latin Vulgate, was intended for use by the common person. Here is the Lord's Prayer in Middle English from the Wycliffe Bible:

> Our Fadir that art in heuenes
> Halewid be thi name
> Thi Kingdom comme to
> Be thi wille done as in heuen so in erthe
> Gyve to us this dai oure breed ouer other
>   substance
> And forgive to us oure dettis
> As we forgyven to oure dettouris
> And leede us not in to temptacioun
> But delyvere us fro yvel[3]

The Middle English of Wycliffe's Lord's Prayer is much easier to understand than the Anglo-Saxon version. The English language was evolving closer to its present form. The influence of Latin is noticeable in this rendition, for instance: *substance* = substantia, *dettis* and *dettouris* = debitum, *temptacioun* = temptatio, *delyvere* = deliberare.

The next English Bible to appear on the scene was translated by William Tyndale. The English language had further matured in the 150 years since the Wycliffe Bible. The Tyndale Bible marked an important step in the progression of English Bible translation. What set Tyndale apart from Wycliffe was not only the freshness of his translation but also his use of Hebrew and Greek manuscripts. This practice of utilizing the most ancient available documents has become the standard method of translation for nearly all other English Bibles that have followed. The Tyndale Bible was also the first English Bible printed on a press.

Like Wycliffe, Tyndale felt that the only way people could understand spiritual concepts was to be able to read the Bible in their own language. In his own words: "Because I had perceaved by experyence, how that it was impossible to stablysh the laye people in any truth, except the scripture were playnly layde before their eyes in their mother tonge, that they might se the processe, ordre and meaninge of the texte."[4]

In the early sixteenth century, the authorized version of the Bible continued to be the thousand-year-old Latin Vulgate. However, English, not Latin, was the language of the people. So, filled with enthusiasm, Tyndale set out to translate the Bible into English. He immediately ran into opposition from the church hierarchy and was compelled to leave England for the friendlier religious climate of Luther's Germany in order to continue his work.[5] While in Germany, Tyndale published the New Testament in 1525, the Pentateuch in 1530, the Book of Jonah in 1531, and a revision of the New Testament in 1534. He also completed the translation of many other Old Testament books but was unable to publish them himself.[6]

Although thousands of Tyndale Bibles were printed, the chaotic political climate of the Protestant Reformation severely limited their distribution among the people. Many were seized and burned by the religious authorities and only fragments survive today. Politics also did not favor Tyndale personally. He never returned to his native England. In 1535 he was kidnapped from the free city of Antwerp and imprisoned at the Vilvorde fortress near Brussels. In 1536 he was condemned for heresy, strangled, and burned at the stake.

Tyndale's martyrdom in no way stopped the flood of English translations that followed. Interestingly, nearly every English Bible published thereafter was essentially a revision of Tyndale's brave work. Some scholars estimate that 70–90 percent of the New Testament from the King James Version is Tyndale. If Gutenberg was the father of Bible publishing, Tyndale was certainly the father of English Bible translation. The Lord's Prayer according to William Tyndale:

> "O oure father which arte in heven,
> halowed be thy name.
> Let thy kyngdome come.
> Thy wyll be fulfilled,
> as well in erth, as it ys in heven.

> Geve vs thisdaye oure dayly breede.
> And forgeve vs oure treaspases,
> even as we forgeve oure trespacers.
> And leade vs not into temptacion:
> but delyver vs from evell.
> For thyne is the kyngedome and the power,
> and the glorye for ever. Amen."[7]

Except for the occasional differences in spelling, Tyndale's Lord's Prayer is nearly the same Lord's Prayer we recite today. Now you know whom to thank for it.

I hope that this excursion into the creation of the English Bible has been interesting and informative. Allow me to re-emphasize the fact that our Bibles are translations, not the original words. Unfortunately, the original biblical writings are long gone. The documents we do have are the best ancient *Xerox equivalents* available (transcribed by hand—if only they were produced on a modern photocopy machine). Unless you are prepared to spend many years learning ancient Hebrew and Greek, then you are stuck reading the Bible in your, as William Tyndale puts it, "mother tonge." Therefore, we are all at the mercy of Bible translators in their accurately rendering these manuscripts into English. Fortunately, we are blessed with many excellent English Bibles from which to choose.

Recommended Bible Translations

You are now ready to pick a Bible translation! In this section, I have included a review of many of the English translations currently available. These versions are recommended based on the following criteria:

(1) The Bible must be an actual translation of the Hebrew, Greek, and Aramaic manuscripts.[8] This requirement ensures that the version you read will come from as close to the source of the original words as possible.

(2) The Bible must be produced by more than one translator. No one person is qualified to translate the Bible alone. What's the saying: *Two heads are better than one?* You wouldn't buy a car built by one person, would you? Why read a Bible translated by one person? What one translator doesn't see in rendering a word or phrase, another will. All the recommended Bibles were translated by a team of translators.

Versions of the Bible that do not meet these two basic standards are not included on the recommended list (some of these Bibles will be discussed later—see "Other Bibles"). For comparison's sake, the Lord's Prayer is included from each version.[9] Here are the recommended versions in chronological order according to their earliest publishing date of the complete Bible:

King James Version (KJV)—1611

Named after the king who commissioned its development, the King James Version (KJV),[10] sometimes known as the Authorized Version (AV), is the only pre-twentieth-century version of the Bible still widely read today. When it was begun in 1604, many different Bibles were in use by various constituencies of Christians. The KJV provided a Bible upon which all members of the English-speaking world could agree. Amazingly, this translation has survived since its unveiling in 1611 all the way into modern times. This durability is perhaps due in part to the excellence of the translation for its day.

Millions of people grew up with the King James Bible and have committed its passages to memory. Its familiarity of verse and poetry are its strong points. The KJV also has its weaknesses, particularly in two areas: (1) the English language has changed significantly in the last 387 years, rendering some of the text archaic to the modern reader, and (2) new manuscripts more ancient than those available to the King James translators have surfaced, revealing errors in their translation. Some editions of the KJV even include other translations in brackets to correct these errors. In spite of its deficiencies, the KJV remains a Bible worth having on your bookshelf as a classic piece of English literature. Some even find it to be their study Bible of choice. The Lord's Prayer (Matthew 6:9–13) according to the KJV:

> "Our Father which art in heaven,
> Hallowed be thy name.
> Thy kingdom come.
> Thy will be done in earth, as it is in heaven.
> Give us this day our daily bread.
> And forgive us our debts,
> as we forgive our debtors.
> And lead us not into temptation,
> but deliver us from evil:
> For thine is the kingdom, and the power, and
> the glory, for ever. Amen."

American Standard Version (ASV)—1901

The first concerted effort to revise the KJV was begun in 1870 by a committee of scholars from both England and the United States. In 1881 the New Testament was completed, with the Old Testament following in 1885. The new Bible came to be called the English Revised Version. Though a major improvement over the KJV, the English Revised Version never caught fire with the British populace. The KJV remained the Bible of choice among the everyday Bible reader.

Across the Atlantic in the United States, the American Standard Version (ASV) made a bit more headway with the reading public. First published in 1901, the ASV was an American version of the English Revised Version, translated with the American reader in mind. Charles Fillmore used the ASV in his writings, particularly in the *Metaphysical Bible*

Dictionary. One notable change in the ASV translation compared with the KJV was the name for God in the Old Testament. The KJV used *Lord;* the ASV used *Jehovah.*[11] The word *Jehovah* was a European attempt to pronounce the Hebrew *YHWH* by adding vowels to it. The more acceptable pronunciation for *YHWH* is "Yahweh."[12] The Lord's Prayer according to the ASV:

> "Our Father who art in heaven,
> Hallowed be thy name.
> Thy kingdom come.
> Thy will be done, as in heaven, so on earth.
> Give us this day our daily bread.
> And forgive us our debts,
> as we also have forgiven our debtors.
> And bring us not into temptation,
> but deliver us from the evil one."

Revised Standard Version (RSV)—1952

The Revised Standard Version (RSV) is a revision of the American Standard Version (ASV). Published fifty years after the ASV, the RSV benefited from the discoveries of better manuscripts and improved translation techniques. It is one of the first Bibles to benefit from the discovery of the Dead Sea Scrolls. One significant change in the RSV over its mother version was the reinstatement of *Lord* for *Jehovah* as the Hebrew word for God. This change was in keeping with the KJV and early Greek and Latin translations of the Old Testament. For example, the opening verse from the 23rd Psalm in the ASV reads, "Jehovah is my shepherd; I shall not want," whereas the RSV reverts to the more familiar "The Lord is my shepherd; I shall not want."

For the most part, the Bible-reading public has welcomed the RSV since its arrival. While it is a modern English translation, it still retains some of the language and poetry of the KJV. The Lord's Prayer according to the RSV:

> "Our Father who art in heaven,
> Hallowed be thy name.
> Thy kingdom come,
> Thy will be done,
>   On earth as it is in heaven.
> Give us this day our daily bread;
> And forgive us our debts,
>   As we also have forgiven our debtors;
> And lead us not into temptation,
>   But deliver us from evil."

The Jerusalem Bible—1966

While the Protestants were busy producing numerous translations of the Bible during the sixteenth century, the Catholics were also in the thick of it themselves. A group of English Catholic scholars moved to France and translated the Bible into English. The result of their efforts was the Douay-Rheims Bible.[13] Unlike the KJV, which followed the Tyndale practice of using Hebrew and Greek documents, the Douay-Rheims Bible followed the Wycliffe tradition of translating the Bible from the Latin Vulgate. Thus the Douay-Rheims Bible contains many errors and uniquely Latinized renderings. The Lord's Prayer according to the Douay-Rheims Bible:

> "Ovr Father which art in heauen,
> sanctified be thy name.
> Let thy Kingdom come.
> Thy wil be done, as in heauen, in earth also.
> Giue vs to day our supersubstantial bread.
> And forgiue vs our dettes,
> as we also forgiue our detters.

And leade vs not into tentation.
But deliuer vs from euil. Amen."[14]

Those of you who grew up as Roman Catholics may recognize the Douay-Rheims Bible. Fortunately, it went through many revisions over the centuries, correcting much of its odd English. However, it still lacked the accuracy of a translation based on original biblical languages and manuscripts. Even in light of this fact, it remained the official English Bible of the Catholic church well into the twentieth century. In the 1940s another translation by Msgr. Ronald A. Knox was authorized by the Catholic hierarchy. Also, like the Douay-Rheims Bible, the Knox version was based on the Latin Vulgate.

The Vatican Council II (1963–65) changed the Catholic biblical climate for the better. The Catholic church finally recognized the validity and superiority of manuscripts other than the Latin Vulgate. The New American Bible (also a good translation) was published in 1970. Even a Catholic edition of the RSV appeared. Also benefiting from this new scholastic environment was The Jerusalem Bible, published in 1966. Originally begun by French Dominican scholars in Jerusalem (hence the name The Jerusalem Bible), The Jerusalem Bible is a fresh, modern English translation from ancient manuscripts. Of all the Bibles produced by Catholics, it is the one most often read by non-Catholics. It also is the only English Bible that translates the Hebrew word for God, *YHWH,* as *Yahweh.* Thus the 23rd Psalm begins, "Yahweh is my shepherd, I lack nothing." The Jerusalem Bible has gone through two revisions (1973 and 1985) since it was first introduced. The Lord's Prayer according to The Jerusalem Bible:

"Our Father in heaven,
    may your name be held holy,
    your kingdom come,
    your will be done,

on earth as in heaven.
Give us today our daily bread.
And forgive us our debts,
as we have forgiven those who are
in debt to us.
And do not put us to the test,
but save us from the evil one."

New English Bible (NEB)—1970

Unlike its predecessors, the English Revised Version, ASV, and RSV, the New English Bible (NEB) was a not a remake of the KJV but a whole new translation. During the twentieth century, the need emerged for a contemporary English-language Bible, free from the antiquated language of the KJV. The initial impetus for this new translation began with the Church of Scotland in 1946 and subsequently developed into a team of scholars from other denominations and organizations throughout the British Isles (including representatives from the Catholic church). In 1961 the New Testament was published, followed by the Old Testament and Apocrypha in 1970.

Like The Jerusalem Bible, the NEB is a contemporary English translation. Gone is most of the old-time biblical lingo of the KJV. Yet at the same time, the NEB does not use slang or colloquialisms that might go out of use in the span of a decade or two. Its English is basic, modern, and understandable. The greatest criticism of the NEB is that its language is not "churchy" enough for some readers. You be the judge. The Lord's Prayer according to the NEB:

"Our Father in heaven,
thy name be hallowed;
thy kingdom come,

thy will be done,
on earth as in heaven.
Give us today our daily bread.
Forgive us the wrong we have done,
as we have forgiven those who have
      wronged us.
And do not bring us to the test,
but save us from the evil one."

New American Standard Bible (NASB)—1971

The New American Standard Bible (NASB), like the RSV, is a revision of the ASV (Enough acronyms for you?). It is the product of the Lockman Foundation of La Habra, California, also the publisher of the Amplified Bible (1965). The NASB improves upon the ASV in that it makes use of more up-to-date manuscripts and renders those manuscripts into a more contemporary English than its turn-of-the-century ancestor. Also, as in the RSV, the Hebrew name for God has been changed from *Jehovah* to *Lord*. The Lord's Prayer according to the NASB:

"Our Father who art in heaven,
Hallowed be Thy name.
Thy kingdom come.
Thy will be done,
On earth as it is in heaven.
Give us this day our daily bread.
And forgive us our debts, as we also have for-
      given our debtors.
And do not lead us into temptation, but
      deliver us from evil. [For Thine is the
      kingdom, and the power, and the glory,
      forever. Amen]."

Today's English Version (TEV)—1976

Today's English Version (TEV), also known as the Good News Bible, is a modern English translation published by the American Bible Society. The language style of the TEV is very contemporary and in no way borrows phrases from traditional versions. For example: Goliath and David's meeting (1 Samuel 17:41–44) in the RSV reads:

> "And the Philistine came on and drew near to David, with his shield-bearer in front of him. And when the Philistine looked, and saw David, he disdained him; for he was but a youth, ruddy and comely in appearance. And the Philistine said to David, 'Am I a dog, that you come to me with sticks?' And the Philistine cursed David by his gods. The Philistine said to David, 'Come to me, and I will give your flesh to the birds of the air and to the beasts of the field.'"

Today's English Version translates this same passage:

> "The Philistine started walking toward David, with his shield bearer walking in front of him. He kept coming closer, and when he got a good look at David, he was filled with scorn for him because he was just a nice, good-looking boy. He said to David, 'What's that stick for? Do you think I'm a dog?' And he called down curses from his god on David. 'Come on,' he challenged David, 'and I will give your body to the birds and animals to eat.'"

The TEV version of this story reads more like a trash-talking street fight than in the just slightly older RSV. Keep in mind, the RSV was a revision of the three-centuries-old KJV, whereas TEV was an entirely new translation with no ties to any former version. Because TEV was written in a simple, almost conversational tone, it lacks much of the poetic beauty of earlier versions. Some people favor this direct style. Another unique feature of this Bible is the numerous line drawings interspersed throughout the text. The Lord's Prayer according to TEV:

> "Our Father in heaven:
> May your holy name be honored;
> may your Kingdom come;
> may your will be done on earth as it is
>   in heaven.
> Give us today the food we need.
> Forgive us the wrongs we have done,
>   as we forgive the wrongs that others
>   have done to us.
> Do not bring us to hard testing,
>   but keep us safe from the Evil One."

New International Version (NIV)—1978

The New International Version (NIV) was truly an *international* effort, involving over a hundred scholars from around the English-speaking world. Sponsored by the New York International Bible Society, the NIV was completed in 1978. Published in the United States by The Zondervan Corporation of Grand Rapids, Michigan, the NIV is an extremely successful Bible with sales well into the millions. What makes the NIV so desirable to many Bible readers is its clear, straightforward, intelligible language.

Consider the description of spiritual faith in Hebrews 11:1. The KJV renders it: "Now faith is the substance of things hoped for, the evidence of things not seen." When I have read this passage, its language has always compelled me to pause for a moment in thought before I began to comprehend its meaning.

Now, read it in the NIV: "Now faith is being sure of what we hope for and certain of what we do not see." Can you see how easily the NIV reads compared with the KJV? Which do you prefer? The Lord's Prayer according to the NIV:

> "Our Father in heaven,
> hallowed be your name,
> your kingdom come,
> your will be done
>   on earth as it is in heaven.
> Give us today our daily bread.
> Forgive us our debts,
>   as we also have forgiven our debtors.
> And lead us not into temptation,
> but deliver us from the evil one."

New King James Version (NKJV)—1982

Nearly one hundred years passed after the English Revised Version (1881–85) before another attempt was made to directly update the KJV. In 1982 the New King James Version (NKJV) debuted on the scene. Utilizing the latest manuscripts, the NKJV corrected the major deficiencies of the KJV while retaining much of the original's literary flavor. Old-fashioned pronouns and verb endings such as *thee, thine,* and *doeth* were modernized into the more commonly used *you, yours,* and *do* of today's English.

Also, current word usage was employed where necessary in order to make passages more understandable. For example, let us compare Paul's well-known speech on the qualities of spiritual love found in 1 Corinthians 13. The first verse from the KJV reads, "Though I speak with the tongues of men and of angels, and have not charity, I am become as sounding brass, or a tinkling cymbal." The NKJV reads almost the same way except with one significant word change: "Though I speak with the tongues of men and of angels, but have not love, I have become as sounding brass or a clanging cymbal."

Did you notice which word was changed the most? No, not "clanging" for "tinkling." The important change was the translation of the word *agape,* the Greek word for spiritual love. The KJV uses "charity" whereas the NKJV uses "love." Today the word *charity* means something entirely different than it did in 1611. We ordinarily associate "charity" with giving to the United Way, the Jerry Lewis Muscular Dystrophy Telethon, or some other worthy cause. Hopefully, love is operative in one's charitable acts. However, "charity" no longer means love. If you grew up with the KJV, you will easily grasp the familiarity of the NKJV. The Lord's Prayer according to the NKJV:

> "Our Father in heaven,
> Hallowed be Your name.
> Your kingdom come.
> Your will be done
> On earth as it is in heaven.
> Give us this day our daily bread.
> And forgive us our debts,
> As we forgive our debtors.
> And do not lead us into temptation,
> But deliver us from the evil one.
> For Yours is the kingdom and the power and the
> glory forever. Amen."

New Revised Standard Version (NRSV)—1989

The New Revised Standard Version (NRSV) is a revision of the RSV, which is a revision of the ASV, which is a revision of the KJV. Let's see, that makes the NRSV a triple revision of the KJV—right? All attempts at humor aside, the NRSV is a

1980s update of the RSV. The NRSV utilizes Hebrew and Greek manuscripts unavailable to the RSV translators, including a more expanded use of the Dead Sea Scrolls. Additionally, the NRSV completely eliminates the archaic speech of the KJV and ASV still present in the RSV. For instance, Psalm 8:1 in the RSV reads, "O Lord, our Lord, how majestic is thy name in all the earth! Thou whose glory above the heavens is chanted." The NRSV reads, "O Lord, our Sovereign, how majestic is your name in all the earth! You have set your glory above the heavens."

The NRSV also eliminates masculine-oriented in favor of gender-inclusive language where the original writers likely meant to include both sexes in the passages. Observe this change in Luke 6:29–31. The RSV reads:

> "To him who strikes you on the cheek, offer the other also; and from him who takes away your coat do not withhold even your shirt. Give to every one who begs from you; and of him who takes away your goods do not ask them again. And as you wish that men would do to you, do so to them."

The NRSV reads:

> "If anyone strikes you on the cheek, offer the other also; and from anyone who takes away your coat do not withhold even your shirt. Give to everyone who begs from you; and if anyone takes away your goods, do not ask for them again. Do to others as you would have them do to you."

The Lord's Prayer according to the NRSV:

> "Our Father in heaven,
>   hallowed be your name.

Your kingdom come.
>Your will be done, on earth as it is in
>heaven.
Give us this day our daily bread.
And forgive us our debts,
>as we also have forgiven our debtors.
And do not bring us to the time of trial,
>but rescue us from the evil one."

Revised English Bible (REB)—1989

Practically all improvements of the NRSV can also be found in the Revised English Bible (REB). The main difference is that the REB is a revision of the NEB, not the RSV. Like the NRSV, the REB updates the NEB in two significant ways:

(1) Although the NEB sparingly uses archaic pronouns such as *thy*, *thee* and *thou*, the REB eliminates them entirely. Let us bring forward the example from the NRSV section, Psalm 8:1. The NEB reads, "O Lord our sovereign, how glorious is thy name in all the earth! Thy majesty is praised high as the heavens." The REB changes the verse to "Lord our sovereign, how glorious is your name throughout the world! Your majesty is praised as high as the heavens."

(2) The Revised English Bible also attempts to use gender-inclusive language where appropriate and feasible. Again, let us compare Luke 6:29–31. The NEB:

> "When a man hits you on the cheek, offer him the other cheek too; when a man takes your coat, let him have your shirt as well. Give to everyone who asks you; when a man takes what is yours, do not demand it back. Treat others as you would like them to treat you."

The REB:

> "If anyone hits you on the cheek, offer the other also; if anyone takes your coat, let him have your shirt as well. Give to everyone who asks you; if anyone takes what is yours, do not demand it back. Treat others as you would like them to treat you."

The Lord's Prayer according to the REB:

> "Our Father in heaven,
>   may your name be hallowed;
>   your kingdom come,
>   your will be done,
>   on earth as in heaven.
>   Give us today our daily bread.
>   Forgive us the wrong we have done,
>   as we have forgiven those who have
>   wronged us.
>   And do not put us to the test,
>   but save us from the evil one."

Summary of the NRSV and REB

Although the NRSV and the REB are certainly not identical translations, I feel it is apropos to recommend these two Bibles together because of the similar intent and style of their revisions. It is almost uncanny that both Bibles were published the same year, 1989. As in any revision of the Bible, thousands of modifications were made to the texts of the NRSV and REB. However, the two previously described changes make the NRSV and the REB attractive to the modern, socially aware Bible reader.

Contemporary English Version (CEV)—1995

Are you looking for a translation that is thoroughly fresh and modern? If so, the Contemporary English Version (CEV) may be just what the doctor ordered. Published by the American Bible Society, the CEV is an attempt to not only translate the Bible with the reader in mind but the listener as well. Archaic, awkward, obsolete, and sexist language is completely eliminated, making the CEV very readable. To quote the translators, "The result [of their work] is an English text that is enjoyable and easily understood by the vast majority of English speakers, regardless of their religious or educational background."

The CEV is a startling translation to read for the first time. I recommend that you browse some familiar passages and compare them with older renditions. You will be surprised how well the CEV lives up to its name. Consider these passages:

> "God said, 'Now we will make humans, and they will be like us. We will let them rule the fish, the birds, and other living creatures.' So God created humans to be like himself; he made men and women."
> (Gen. 1:26–27)

> "You, Lord, are my shepherd.
> I will never be in need.
> You let me rest in fields
>   of green grass.
> You lead me to streams
>   of peaceful water,
>   and you refresh my life."
> —Psalm 23:1–3

The Lord's Prayer according to the CEV:

> "Our Father in heaven,
>   help us to honor your name.
> Come and set up your kingdom,
>   so that everyone on earth will obey you,
>   as you are obeyed in heaven.
> Give us our food for today.
> Forgive us for doing wrong,
>   as we forgive others.
> Keep us from being tempted
>   and protect us from evil."

The Jewish Publication Society of America— 1963–82

One of the finest English translations of the Hebrew Bible (Old Testament) is published by the Jewish Publication Society of America. Their original translation was issued in 1917 and since has been followed with an updated version in three volumes: The Torah: The First Five Books of Moses (Genesis–Deuteronomy) in 1963; The Prophets-Nevi'im (Joshua–II Kings, Isaiah, Jeremiah, Ezekiel, and the 12 Minor Prophets) in 1978; The Writings-Kethubim (the remaining books of the Hebrew scriptures) in 1982.[15] The translators improved upon their earlier work by availing themselves of the most recent advances in biblical scholarship and by smoothly rendering the idiomatic nature of the Hebrew text into an understandable English. For obvious reasons, the 23rd Psalm has been substituted for the Lord's Prayer:

> "The Lord is my shepherd;
>   I lack nothing.

He makes me lie down in green pastures;
    He leads me to water in places of
        repose;
    He renews my life;
    He guides me in right paths as befits
        His name.
Though I walk through a valley of deepest
        darkness,
    I fear no harm, for You are with me;
    Your rod and Your staff—they comfort me.

You spread a table for me in full view of my
        enemies;
    You anoint my head with oil;
    my drink is abundant.
Only goodness and steadfast love shall
        pursue me
    all the days of my life,
    and I shall dwell in the house of the Lord
    for many long years."

Other Bibles

Included in this chapter are a few Bibles not recommended for serious Bible study. They are versions that do not stand up to each of the recommended Bible study standards. Allow me to refresh your memory of them: (1) the Bible must be an actual translation of the Hebrew, Greek, and Aramaic manuscripts and (2) the Bible must be produced by more than one translator. You may ask, why mention them at all? In spite of their shortcomings, these Bibles can often bring a fresh, new perspective when comparing them with other versions. They are also interesting reading.

Phillips Modern English Bible—1947–72

The Phillips Modern English Bible is a contemporary translation of the New Testament. Although this version is a translation of the ancient manuscripts, it was translated by only one person, J. B. Phillips. Phillips began translating the New Testament in the 1940s and continued revising his work into the 1970s. His translations of Paul's Epistles read refreshingly like the conversational letters that they originally were. The Lord's Prayer according to the Phillips Modern English Bible:

> "Our Heavenly Father, may your name be
> honoured;
> May your kingdom come, and your will be
> done on earth as it is in Heaven.
> Give us each day the bread we need for the
> day,
> Forgive us what we owe to you, as we have
> also forgiven those who owe anything
> to us.
> Keep us clear of temptation, and save us
> from evil."

The Lamsa Bible—1957

The controversy surrounding the Lamsa Bible, as it is often called, (mentioned in Chapter 4), centers on Lamsa's claim that the Peshitta,[16] the source material of his translation, is the most ancient and, therefore, the most authoritative Bible manuscript. Consequently, he maintains that Aramaic, not Hebrew and Greek, was the original language of the entire Bible.

Though George Lamsa was surely well meaning in his convictions, he stands alone in the world of biblical scholarship. Most scholars point out that the Peshitta is a Syriac[17] translation of the Bible from the original Hebrew and Greek manuscripts. This version dates from the early centuries C.E. and not the earlier date that George Lamsa asserts. On the basis of this observation, the Lamsa Bible might be considered on a par with, say, the Douay-Rheims translation of the Latin Vulgate. Because the Lamsa Bible does not meet either of the requirements for recommended study, it is included in this section. The Lord's Prayer according to the Lamsa Bible:

> "Our Father in heaven.
> Hallowed be thy name.
> Thy kingdom come.
> Let thy will be done, as in heaven so on earth.
> Give us bread for our needs from day to day.
> And forgive us our offences, as we have
>   forgiven our offenders;
> And do not let us enter into temptation,
> but deliver us from error.
> Because thine is the kingdom and the power
>   and the glory for ever and ever.
>   Amen."

The Living Bible (TLB)—1971

Also known as *The Book* and *The Way*, The Living Bible (TLB) is the Bible most often found in your local supermarket. Since it was first published in 1971, TLB is one of the most successful versions of the Bible, with billions of copies in print. What distinguishes this Bible from most is that it is a paraphrase, not a translation, and thus disqualifies itself from the recommended list. Paraphrasing can be helpful in quickly conveying the meaning of a writer's words, thus speeding the pace of reading. The danger of paraphrasing is that it tends to be more subject to editorializing and interpretation than actual translation. The Living Bible, admittedly, was written with an evangelical bent.[18] The Lord's Prayer according to TLB:

> "Our Father in heaven,
>   we honor your holy name.
> We ask that your kindgom will come now.
> May your will be done here on earth, just as it is
>   in heaven.
> Give us food again today, as usual,
> and forgive us our sins,
> just as we have forgiven those who have sinned
>   against us.
> Don't bring us into temptation,
> but deliver us from the Evil One. Amen."

The Reader's Digest Bible—1982

Another paraphrase of the Bible is the Readers' Digest Bible. Based on the RSV, the writers at Reader's Digest employed their talents of book condensation to produce a Bible that was shorter and easier to read. How much shorter? According to their estimates, the Old Testament was shrunk by 50 percent, and the New Testament by 25 percent, making the entire Bible 40 percent shorter. If a person's sole interest is to read the basic story line of the Bible without regard to individual verses (verse numbers have been removed), the Reader's Digest Bible will suffice. The Lord's Prayer according to the Reader's Digest Bible is identical to the RSV.

Future English Translations

As long as the English language changes, new manuscripts are discovered, better translation methods are developed, and people still want to read the Bible, then new translations will be published. The twentieth century has produced more translations than any other century. Who knows what the twenty-first century will bring for Bible translation?

Bible Editions

Bibles come in all shapes and sizes, and/or, editions. An edition of a Bible is determined by its layout or format. It's like a plate of pasta. If we think of the Bible translation as the noodles, the sauce is the edition. Regardless of which sauce (edition) is poured on top, the noodles (translation) underneath remain constant. In a way, the edition of your Bible is almost as important as the translation, just as marinara or alfredo sauce is essential to making the pasta dish desirable to eat. Let's say you may have a copy of the NRSV, but if the print is too small or if there are no study aids, you may be less inclined to read it. A good edition can make a Bible more inviting, encouraging, and useful to its readers.

A case in point: you've decided to read the book of Amos but have no idea what the book is about. Who was Amos? When did he live? What are the book's main points? An edition of the Bible that includes explanatory study notes would instantly answer these questions. Just as pasta is best served with sauce, the best study Bibles are those that contain more than the desired translation.

What kind of sauce should you have on your pasta? That is, what should you look for in a study edition of the Bible? The choices are many. Consider these editions:

Bible Edition	Translations	Features	Publisher
HarperCollins Study Bible	NRSV	A, B, C, F, H, I	HarperCollins
Life Application Bible	KJV, NIV, NKJV, NRSV	A, B, C, F, G, H, I, J, K	World/Tyndale
Master Study Bible	NASB	D, E, F, H, K	Holman
NIV Study Bible	NIV	B, C, D, F, G, H, I, J	Zondervan
NRSV Harper Study Bible	NRSV	B, C, D, F, H, J	Zondervan
Oxford Study Edition	RSV, NEB, NRSV, REB	A, B, C, F, H, I , J	Oxford
Ryrie Study Bible	KJV, NASB, NIV	A, B, C, D, F, H, I, J, K	Moody
Scofield Reference	KJV, NASB, NIV	A, B, C, F, H, I, J	Oxford & World
Thompson Chain-Reference	NASB, NIV	A, B, C, D, E, F, G, H, I, J, K	Zondervan

Key to Features

A. Bible chronology outlining the important events of biblical history

B. Introductory notes to each biblical book explaining its authorship, purpose, etc.

C. Comprehensive in-text study notes providing information germane to the text

D. Concordance of important words with corresponding biblical references

E. Dictionary of biblical names, places, and terms

F. Maps detailing the Holy Land of various time periods

G. Charts outlining specific biblical points

H. In-text cross references suggesting other verses for comparison

I. Map index showing where to find certain places on the maps

J. Subject or topical index showing where to find certain subjects in the text

K. Harmony of The Gospels organizes the events of The Gospels into sequence

The Bible editions chart above is by no means perfect. Its information is derived from an informal survey of two Christian bookstores, a municipal library, a small college library, and the author's personal library. I have displayed it here to give you a feel for what is likely available in your community.

Selecting a Good Study Bible

At this point, you may feel totally confused about which Bible to purchase. It may seem that there are too many versions, too many editions, too many choices. My rationale in presenting such an abundance of information is to be as thorough as possible within the scope of this book. As unbelievable as it sounds, the Bibles mentioned in this chapter are only the tip of the Bible-publishing iceberg.

One of the first questions that may cross your mind is whether your current Bible is sufficient for your Bible study needs. After all, there's no sense spending money you don't have to. Here is an easy way to determine if your Bible is up to snuff. First, pick up your present Bible and read through its introductory pages. This may be the first time you've read this part of your Bible. This section will explain the background of your particular edition of the Bible and which translation is provided. Second, search for a few of your favorite Bible stories and verses from the Old and New Testaments. Do you like the way they read? Do you want to read any further? Is the print big enough? Are study notes or maps included? Does your Bible have a quick-reference concordance or dictionary? If your answer is yes to all of these questions, your present Bible may be perfect for your study needs. If not, you are now in the market for a new Bible.

Chances are your Bible is lacking in some way, and you are ready to purchase a new one. How should you go about it? Armed with the information in this chapter, head for the Bible section of your local bookstore. Christian bookstores generally have the best selection of Bibles. Major bookstores such as B. Dalton and Waldenbooks also carry Bibles. Look for these things:

(1) The translation is among the recommended list:

King James Version (KJV)
American Standard Version (ASV)
Revised Standard Version (RSV)
Jerusalem Bible or New American Bible (Catholic Bibles)
New English Bible (NEB)
New American Standard Bible (NASB)
Today's English Version (TEV)
New International Version (NIV)
New King James Version (NKJV)
New Revised Standard Version (NRSV)
Revised English Bible (REB)
Contemporary English Version (CEV)
The Jewish Publication Society of America Hebrew Scriptures

(2) The translation is acceptable to your literary taste. That is, you easily comprehend the language style of the Bible.

(3) The print is large enough for you to read.

(4) The edition of the Bible that offers an assortment of study helps—notes, maps, and other references. Just be-

cause an edition has more features than another does not necessarily make it better. Read through the introductions, notes, maps, indexes, and so forth. Does the philosophy of the edition match yours? If the edition you like does not have a concordance or dictionary, don't fret. You can purchase them separately.

(5) The Bible "feels right." Check your intuition. Or, before you buy, consider test driving a few Bibles from your public library (six of the fourteen recommended Bibles reviewed in this chapter were borrowed from libraries). Buy a Bible you will feel great about owning!

(6) By the way, plan to spend at least $30–$50. If that is sticker shock to you, shop some used bookstores and community book sales. The Bibles will be older, but the prices may be as low as a few dollars.

Audio- & Videocassette Bible

Scripture is not limited to the printed word alone. Complete Bibles are available on audiocassette tape for the visually impaired and for those who prefer to relax and listen to someone else read. Some are even narrated by famous actors such as Charlton Heston and Gregory Peck. Videotapes of better-known Bible stories are also on the market.

Computer Bible

Computers are now a part of our everyday lives. They are incredibly good at processing enormous amounts of information in almost a split second of time. Consequently, they are well suited to the immense nature of the Bible. Bible software is now available in all computer formats including DOS, Macintosh, Windows, and CD-ROM.

Using a computer Bible depends on who you are, your inclinations, resources, and needs. There are advantages and disadvantages to them. It's much like the difference between adding numbers with a calculator or using a pencil and paper. A calculator is quick and accurate. Some people use calculators exclusively. Pencil and paper are slower but often quite satisfactory for some calculations.

Computer Bibles are in their element when searching for specific verses or words. Just click your mouse a few times and the information you want is displayed in a matter of seconds (computer concordances will be discussed in Chapter 6). The same process of using a printed Bible and concordance is sometimes an adventure and takes considerably more time. Computer Bibles, in addition to offering translations and concordances, also feature study editions, dictionaries, atlases, and ancient Hebrew and Greek text. Computers have definitely changed the way we study the Bible.[19]

However, there are times when a hard copy Bible is preferable, especially if your eyes are fried from staring at a video screen all day. Printed Bibles do not require electricity. Specialized training is not needed to use them. Also, computers are bulkier, whereas printed Bibles can be carried anywhere.[20]

Summary

From ancient manuscripts to computer software, from Anglo-Saxon to modern English, the Bible has come a long way in its evolution. It is my hope that the information in this chapter has been helpful in demystifying the subject of Bible translation and has provided you with some practical tips on how to purchase an appropriate Bible for your study needs. Remember, the translation you select will influence your interpretation of Truth in the Bible. Happy shopping!

Notes

1. Matthew 7:24, 26.

2. Ira Maurice Price, *The Ancestry of Our English Bible,* 2d ed. (Philadelphia: The Sunday School Times Company, 1907), p. 228.

3. Ibid.

4. From *God's Word Into English,* by Dewey M. Beegle, Wm. B. Eerdmans Publishing Co., Copyright © 1960, p. 124.

5. Tyndale met Luther in Wittenberg. Like Tyndale, Luther translated the Bible into his native tongue.

6. Tyndale translated Joshua through 11 Chronicles from his prison cell. He later entrusted the work of finishing the Old Testament to a friend and scholar, John Rogers. This later work of Tyndale and Rogers appeared in the Matthew Bible of 1537.

7. F. F. Bruce, *History of the Bible in English* (New York: Oxford University Press, 1978), p. 46.

8. Portions of the Old Testament were originally written in Aramaic, specifically: Jeremiah 10:11, Ezra 4:8—6:18, 7:12–26, and Daniel 2:4—7:28.

9. Some versions of the Bible omit the final phrase from Matthew 6:13 of the Lord's Prayer ("for thine is the Kingdom," etc.). They are not considered to be the words of Jesus, but a later addition to the prayer perhaps inspired by 1 Chronicles 29:11–13 and/or Psalm 72:19.

10. Throughout this book, some versions of the Bible will be referred to by a specific acronym, i.e., KJV = King James Version, RSV = Revised Standard Version. These acronyms will be introduced prior to their use.

11. *Jehovah* appears just seven times in the KJV.

12. *YHWH* is the unutterable word for God among orthodox Jews. The word *adonai* is substituted for reading purposes. *Jehovah* is a combination of the consonants *YHWH* and the vowels from *adonai.*

13. Although the Old Testament was completed first, the New Testament was published at Rheims in 1582. The Old Testament was published at Douay (also spelled, Douai) in 1609–10. Hence the name, Douay-Rheims Bible.

14. Bruce, p. 118.

15. In 1985, these three volumes were condensed into one book called *Tanakh—The Holy Scriptures*.

16. Peshitta, meaning "simple," is the Bible of Syrian Christians and is considered to be the first translation of the entire Bible into the vernacular (150 c.e.).

17. Ancient languages can be confusing to us English-speaking people. Syriac is a derivative of Aramaic. Aramaic is related to Hebrew and was the language of Palestine at the time of Jesus.

18. There is also a new edition of The Living Bible, a blend with the time-honored King James Version, called the New Living Translation.

19. The following translations are available on computer software: KJV, ASV, NASB, New Jerusalem, NIV, NKJV, NRSV, RSV, and TLB. Here are some popular Bible software companies (in alphabetical order): BIBLESOFT, Candlelight Publishing, Harvest PC Bible, Kirkbride Technology, logos, NAVPRESS Software, Parsons, Time Warner Interactive Group, and Zondervan. Shareware is also available for the Bible. Prices generally range from $20 to $150 and can be purchased by mail-order, at computer software stores, and Christian bookstores.

20. Portable laptop computers are now the rage. Many are the size and weight of an average study Bible. Also, Franklin Electronic Publishers puts out a portable electronic Bible that is as small as a handheld calculator.

Chapter 6

Making a Bible Study Tool Kit

N ow that you have your new Bible, you have probably already started reading it. Good! Dig in! Do you
remember the last new car you bought? During that
first week of ownership, did you go out in the driveway,
sit in the car, and inhale the aroma of its new uphol-
stery? Maybe you drove it around the block a few times,
even if you had nowhere to go. Every day this week, sit
down for a few minutes and leaf through your new
Bible. Check out the pictures and the maps. Fan its
pages across your face, and smell the freshness of the
paper. Read a few random verses, just for the heck of it.
Get acquainted with your new friend. The only difference between your new Bible and any new car you may
own is that you'll be reading your Bible long after you've
traded in the car.

As you begin to explore your Bible a little deeper, you
may run into a few difficulties in reading. Perhaps you are
unsuccessful in looking up some old, familiar verses. You
may stumble across a few words you don't know or read a
story that doesn't make sense to you. Even the most-skilled
Bible student has these challenges. Study editions of the
Bible can be helpful in quickly answering many questions,
but because of size constraints, they have their limitations.
This chapter suggests using several additional tools that

will help you in overcoming these common Bible-reading problems.

Bible Concordances

What is a Bible concordance? Essentially, a Bible concordance is a biblical word book. It is a book of words from the Bible organized with specific scriptural references. Why is it so useful? Here's why. For instance, a certain Bible verse keeps running around in your head. Let's say, it's the one about being "transformed by the renewing of your minds." You like this concept and would like to read more about it in your new Bible. The problem is, you can't seem to remember the whole verse, nor where it is located. What do you do? Bible concordance to the rescue!

> **"Bring the full tithe into the storehouse, so that there may be food in my house, and thus put me to the test, says the Lord of hosts; see if I will not open the windows of heaven for you and pour down for you an overflowing blessing."**
>
> —Malachi 3:10

How do you use a Bible concordance to find this passage? Take the key words from the phrase, *transformed, renewing,* and *mind,* and look them up in your concordance. The more unique the word, the easier it will be to find the desired verse. More common words can appear in thousands of verses. In this case, the KJV uses *transformed* just three times, *renewing* twice, and *mind* ninety-five times. Your best bet would be to look up *transformed* or *renewing* to find your long, lost verse. Bingo! The verse is Romans 12:2.

It is important that you use a concordance that is compatible with your version of the Bible. The reason for this is fairly obvious. Each translation uses slightly different words to render the same passage. The words of a concordance must match the words in the Bible. For instance, a KJV concordance goes with a KJV Bible. That same concordance may work to a degree with those Bibles based on the KJV, particularly earlier revisions such as the ASV, but not perfectly. Because of its seventeenth-century language, a KJV concordance may be pretty useless with more contemporary translations. Observe these variations in our phrase from Romans 12:2:

Recommended Bibles

KJV: "but be ye transformed by the renewing of your mind"
ASV: "but be ye transformed by the renewing of your mind"
RSV: "but be transformed by the renewal of your mind"
Jerusalem: "but let your behavior change, modelled by your new mind"
TEV: "but let God transform you inwardly by a complete change of your mind"
NEB: "but let your minds be remade and your whole nature thus transformed"
NIV: "but be transformed by the renewing of your mind"
NKJV: "but be transformed by the renewing of your mind"
NRSV: "but be transformed by the renewing of your minds"
REB: "but be transformed by the renewal of your minds"
CEV: "but let God change the way you think"

Other Bibles

TLB: "but be a new and different person with a fresh newness in all you do and think"
Phillips: "but let God re-make you so that your whole attitude of mind is changed"
Lamsa: "but be transformed by the renewing of your minds"

There are some similarities between the translations. However, the only major word common to each of the recommended Bibles is *mind*(s). The Living Bible doesn't use *mind* at all. *Transformed* is also rendered *behavior change, be new and different*, and *re-make. Renewing* becomes *renewal, new, change, remade, fresh newness*, and *attitude change*. With all of these differing words, you can see the importance of using a concordance that is based on your Bible's particular translation. If you happen to have a concordance that does not match your translation, find one that does. In the meantime, use a thesaurus to look up synonyms for the words you want to find.

Another use for concordances is for finding certain subjects in the Bible. For example, you want to read verses about *love*.

"Your light shall shine brightly to all the ends of the earth."
—Tobit 13:11

To scan through the Bible page by page looking for *love* would take an excessive and unnecessary amount of time. Stop looking for love in all the wrong places, and let your Bible concordance guide you to all the right ones! Incidentally, *love* is found in over three hundred verses.

The first English Bible concordance was published by organist and theologian John Marbeck in 1550. Other concordances have followed. One pre-twentieth-century concordance still in use today is *Cruden's Complete Concordance* (1737). This concordance, based on the KJV, was published by Alexander Cruden, an eighteenth-century Scottish bookshop owner in London.

The best-known concordance is *Strong's Exhaustive Concordance of the Bible* (1890). Written by Dr. James Strong, a professor at Drew Theological Seminary during the latter part of the nineteenth century, this concordance still stands today as the standard by which all concordances are judged. Without the use of computers, Strong produced a concordance that covers every single word and verse in the KJV. A *Strong's Exhaustive Concordance of the Bible* is a must for the serious Bible student.

The main deficiency of both *Cruden's* and *Strong's* concordances for the modern Bible student is that their use is limited to the KJV. Both have undergone revisions over the years, sometimes supplementing words from the English Revised Version and the ASV. As previously mentioned, KJV concordances can be useful with versions of the Bible based on the

1611 classic. Fortunately, other concordances based on modern translations are available.

There are three types of Bible concordances:

(1) Concordances in the back of Bibles. Because they are a
part of the Bible, these concordances are handy to use
and always match the translation of your Bible. Their
main drawback is that they are not very comprehensive
and leave out many helpful words and listings.

(2) Separate book concordances. These concordances are
far more extensive than the "back-of-the-Bible" variety.
They come in many different editions: (a) exhaustive
concordances contain practically every word in the
Bible. These editions are big and heavy, but never fail in
helping you find a verse. (b) concise or popular editions
eliminate many common words and condense the listing
of others to produce a more manageable, user-friendly
book. These editions are well suited to general Bible
study, and (c) compact concordances are even smaller
and very convenient to use and carry.

(3) Computer concordances. Almost all computers have
Bible software concordances built into their programs.
These concordances thrive in the computer environment. Just enter a word or phrase, and in a matter of a
few seconds the program locates every verse containing
them.[1] Once the list of verses is displayed on the video
screen, you can select any verse you wish to see and
even scroll to each instance throughout the Bible.

The advantage of computer concordances over books is
their incredible speed and ease of use. If you presently have a
computer, you may wish to add a Bible program as soon as you
can. You'll be impressed with how well it works. If you don't yet
own a computer, when you eventually do, make sure a Bible
program is among your first software purchases.[2]

Concordances:

Help you **FIND WORDS** in the Bible.
Help you **FIND PASSAGES** in the Bible.
Help you **FIND SUBJECTS** in the Bible.
Work best when they **MATCH YOUR BIBLE
    TRANSLATION.**

Bible Dictionaries

In the course of reading a newspaper, magazine, or book, we occasionally run across words we simply do not com-

> **"The true beginning
> of wisdom is the desire
> to learn."**
> —Wisdom of Solomon 6:17

prehend. When this happens, we either (a) ignore the word and continue reading, (b) act like we know the word and read on, (c) pause for a moment and look up the word in a dictionary before resuming our reading. The choices we make are determined by the urgency of time, personal motivation, and our degree of intellectual egotism.

There is no shame in using a dictionary. How else are you going to learn words you don't know? This attitude especially applies to reading the Bible. When you encounter a word or name in the Bible that is unfamiliar, consult a Bible dictionary.[3] Even if a word is familiar, your knowledge of it may only be cursory. Bible dictionaries not only define words, they explain them in detail.

In your wanderings through your new Bible, you may have read as far as Genesis 16. If you haven't read this chapter yet, do so now. The chapter is about the birth of Ishmael, Abraham's first son. You may wonder, who was Ishmael? He's not a well-known biblical personage like Moses, David, or Peter. A Bible dictionary can help you fill in the blanks regarding Abraham's Ishmael as well as the other five Ishmaels of the Bible.[4] *Peloubet's Bible Dictionary* describes Ishmael:

Ish'mael (ish'ma-el) *(may God hear)*. 1. The son of Abraham by Hagar the Egyptian, his concubine; born when Abraham was fourscore and six years old. Gen. 16:15, 16. (B.C. 1910). Ishmael was the first-born of his father. He was born in Abraham's house when he dwelt in the plain of Mamre; and on the institution of the covenant of circumcision, was circumcised, he being then thirteen years old. Gen. 17:25. With the institution of the covenant, God renewed his promise respecting Ishmael. He does not again appear in the narrative until the weaning of Isaac. . . . Of the later life of Ishmael we know little. He was present with Isaac at the burial of Abraham. He died at the age of 137 years. Gen. 25:17, 18. The sons of Ishmael peopled the north and west of the Arabian peninsula, and supposedly formed the chief element of the Arab nation, the wandering Bedouin tribes. They are now mostly Mohammedans, who look to him as their spiritual father, as the Jews look to Abraham.[5]

Like concordances, Bible dictionaries come in all shapes and sizes, from compact paperbacks to multiple-volume editions. They are included in some study Bibles and computer software. I recommend that you have at least one substantial single-volume Bible dictionary in your library. Abingdon, Doubleday, Holman, Nelson, Oxford, Zondervan, and many other companies publish excellent Bible dictionaries.

More serious Bible students may wish to invest in a multiple-volume dictionary. Two of the better-known ones are *The Anchor Bible Dictionary* (Doubleday) and *The Interpreter's Dictionary of the Bible* (Abingdon). These dictionaries go into considerable depth explaining the meaning, background, textual relationship, and spiritual implications of a particular word or name.

We have all heard the saying, *"a picture is worth a thousand words."* Other special features of most Bible dictionaries are their photographs, drawings, charts, and maps. It is interesting to read about the Garden of Gethsemane or the walls of Jericho, but a photograph of them and your own imagination can take you there. Pictures catch our eyes and impact us in ways words cannot. Can you imagine watching a television news show without videotaped footage of the story the announcer is describing? Most Bible dictionaries also include photographs of archaeological artifacts of particular interest to Bible students.

Bible dictionaries:

Help you **UNDERSTAND WORDS.**
Help you **UNDERSTAND NAMES.**
Help you **UNDERSTAND PLACES.**
Help you **EXPLAIN THEIR MEANING IN DETAIL.**

Bible Commentaries

You are reading the book of Ezekiel, Chapter 37. As you finish the chapter, your mind is filled with many puzzling questions. What do the dry bones represent, and how can they come back to life? Was Ezekiel talking about the resurrection of the dead? What do the two sticks mean? Who was Ephraim? How could David have become king again when he was already dead?

In an effort to answer your own questions, you read the in-text study notes provided in your Bible. The notes are helpful but brief, and your curiosity cries for more information. You need answers. What do you do now? Welcome to the world of Bible commentaries! Where study notes end, commentaries begin. These books provide in-depth, scholastically sound information about what's really going on in each verse, chapter, and book of the Bible.

Bible commentaries are subject to the interpretive bent of their authors. Some contain theological viewpoints that may differ from yours. The best ones are those that offer the least amount of sectarianism and the greatest amount of scholasticism. When using a commentary, look for the answers to your specific questions and leave behind those ideas you find unusable. Again, as with all book purchases, be discriminating.

Bible commentaries, like Bible dictionaries, come in single- and multiple-volume editions. *The Anchor Bible* (Doubleday) and *The Interpreter's Bible* (Abingdon) are two of the best multiple-volume Bible commentaries.[6] Other popular multiple-volume editions include *Basic Bible Commentary* (Abingdon) and *The Daily Study Bible Series* (Westminster). Single-volume commentaries include: *The Interpreter's One-Volume Commentary on the Bible* and *Harper's Bible Commentary* as well as many others.

What about those nagging questions regarding Ezekiel 37? The Interpreter's Bible, Volume VI answers this way:

> Q: What do the dry bones represent, and how can they come back to life?
>
> A: "The vision here described is one of the best-known parts of the book. The dry bones symbolize the Israelites in exile. Yahweh's query, 'Can these bones live?' (vs. 3), doubtless reflects a question often on the tongues of the exiles. The oracle promises the resurrection of the nation. When the prophet prophesied, the bones came together and breath entered the corpses, and they became a great living host. The author may be suggesting that the prophesying of the return will in some sense effect the return."[7]
>
> Q: Was Ezekiel talking about the resurrection of the dead?
>
> A: "The oracle does not imply belief in the gen-

eral resurrection of the dead. . . . It refers to the resurrection of the community of Israel, i.e., to its return to Palestine."[8]

Q: What do the two sticks mean?

A: "The very nature of the symbolism of the dramatic action in the oracle of the two sticks (vss. 15–28) implies the editor's theme of the restoration of Israel and Judah under Yahweh's servant, the Davidic Messiah."[9]

Q: Who was Ephraim?

A: "The tribes associated with Ephraim are the other nine tribes of the Northern Kingdom."[10]

Q: How could David have become king when he was already dead?

A: "The editor as usual designates the king as prince (cf. 37:25; 44:3; 46:2, 4, 8; etc.). He is described also as my servant, even as David himself is designated in II Sam. 3:18—7:5; II Kings 8:19; etc. . . . There is not an allusion here to the resurrection of the historic David, although the passage has been so interpreted. . . . This figure is . . . not a king who will live forever, but the restorer of the dynasty."[11]

Bible commentaries:

Help you **UNDERSTAND INDIVIDUAL VERSES.**
Help you **UNDERSTAND BIBLE STORIES.**
Help you **UNDERSTAND BIBLICAL BOOKS.**
Help you **EXPLAIN WHAT IS REALLY HAPPENING.**

Bible Atlases

Oh where, oh where, can Bethlehem be? All of us are familiar with the fabled city of Jesus' birth. The Christmas story tells us about Joseph and Mary's long journey from Nazareth, the lack of accommodations at the inn, and the makeshift birthing room in a stable. Where precisely is Bethlehem?

Let's say we are also interested in the location of Bethlehem . . . Pennsylvania that is. What would you do to find that lesser-known city by the same name? You would probably consult an atlas. The index of the atlas shows you the map and coordinates of any city you wish to find. A quick look reveals that Bethlehem, Pennsylvania, is north of Philadelphia and just a few miles northeast of Allentown across the Lehigh River. So, how do you find the original Bethlehem? You use exactly the same procedure with one exception—make sure you are using a Bible atlas.

"All the works of the Lord are good, and he supplies every need as it occurs."
—Ecclesiasticus 39:33

One characteristic of Bible atlases absent from today's atlases is their maps of different time periods. This is a necessity, given the political changes that have taken place in the Middle East over the last 3000–4000 years. Cities were born, flourished, changed names, and occasionally withered away into near oblivion. A case in point:

The ancient city of Shechem was a key city in Palestine for thousands of years. The Canaanites first inhabited the city, followed later by the Jews. Many important biblical events took place there. Abraham heard God's promise of inheriting the land while in Shechem and, subsequently, built an altar there. Jacob bought some land in Shechem. Jacob's sons, Simeon and Levi, killed the men of Shechem to avenge the rape of their sister Dinah. Joseph's body was buried in the lot that Jacob had bought in Shechem. Abimelech, son of Gideon, set himself up as a king in Shechem, only later to destroy the city. Jeroboam I, the first king of the Northern Kingdom of Israel, made Shechem his capital. During Old Testament times, Shechem was a happening place.

On most biblical maps, Shechem shows up as a city in the hill country of central Palestine about thirty miles north of

Jerusalem with Mount Ebal to the north and Mount Gerizim to the south. However, on later maps, Shechem disappears. What happened? The New Testament does not mention Shechem by name.[12] Some sources report that after one of its rebuilding projects, Shechem was renamed Flavia Neapolis, or Neapolis, in honor of the Roman Emperor Flavius Vespasian.[13] Neapolis continues today as the bustling Palestinian city of Nablus. Such is the long history of Shechem.

Your Bible's maps may be sufficient for your study needs, especially those with map indexes that direct you to specific locations. If your Bible is lacking in this area, you might consider adding a Bible atlas to your tool chest. Oxford and Reader's Digest publish excellent Bible atlases that also feature photographs and descriptions of various biblical sites. Computer Bible atlases are also available.

Now, where is Bethlehem? Did you find it yet? It is located in the Judean hill country approximately six miles south of Jerusalem.

Bible atlases:

Help you **LOCATE CITIES.**
Help you **LOCATE LAKES.**
Help you **LOCATE RIVERS.**
Help you **LOCATE VALLEYS.**
Help you **LOCATE MOUNTAINS OF THE BIBLE.**

Bible Handbooks

Wisdom for a Lifetime has been tailored to a specific audience and speaks to a biblical approach relevant to that group. However, many other Bible handbooks, written with a broader audience in mind, can be quite useful to the metaphysical Christian. They offer general information about the books of the Bible, biblical themes, and religious history. Bible handbooks often include timelines, charts, maps, photographs, and other helpful information. Many handbooks suggest interpretative approaches.

In some ways, the information in Bible handbooks resembles that in study Bibles, dictionaries, commentaries, and atlases. All contain biblical information. However, there are differences. Study Bibles are good for quick reference but are limited by space constraints. Dictionaries are geared toward answering questions about specific names, places, and terms. Commentaries tend to focus on a verse-by-verse interpretation. Bible handbooks have the advantage of putting together many of the elements of each biblical study tool into one easy-to-use volume. If you decide to buy just one Bible study tool, a Bible handbook would be your best choice. If you plan to obtain all the biblical tools mentioned in this chapter, a Bible handbook is nice to have on your tool belt.[14]

> **"For mortals it is impossible, but for God all things are possible."**
> —Matthew 19:26

Some excellent Bible handbooks include *Abingdon Bible Handbook, Eerdman's Handbook to the Bible, Halley's Bible Handbook* (Zondervan), and *The Oxford Companion to the Bible.*

Bible handbooks:

Help you **OBTAIN GENERAL BIBLE INFORMATION.**
Help you **UNDERSTAND BIBLE HISTORY.**
Help you **GRASP RELIGIOUS TERMINOLOGY.**
Help you **PROPOSE POSSIBLE INTERPRETATIONS.**

Other Helpful and Interesting Books

There is not always a clear distinction among the various tools of Bible study, as we have seen with Bible handbooks.

Some books present many tools in one package. Others offer ideas that are unique unto themselves. The number of Bible books is seemingly endless. Just name the subject, and there are Bible books published about it.[15] Here is a small sample of what is available:

Bible picture books
Bible pronunciation guides
Bible stories
Bible study group guides
Bible textbooks
Black Bible commentaries
Profiles of Bible characters
Roget's Thesaurus of the Bible
Women's Bible commentaries
Works of Josephus

Buying a Basic Bible Tool Kit

Concordances: Prices vary from $5 (compact) up to $40 (exhaustive). You should be able to pick up a popular/concise edition for around $15–$20. Important: Make sure you buy one that matches your version of the Bible. Again, serious Bible students should have a *Strong's Exhaustive Concordance of the Bible* in their library.

Dictionaries: Single-volume dictionaries can be purchased for about the same price as a similarly sized concordance. These are usually sufficient for most students. Multiple-volume dictionaries, costing in the hundreds of dollars, are excellent for in-depth study.

Commentaries: Single-volume commentaries go for $30–$40. Multiple-volume sets range from $130–$1700, depending upon the publisher. One should have a single- or a multiple-volume commentary in his or her Bible study tool kit.

Atlases: These are usually the least expensive of the Bible study tools. Prices start as low as $5. Review the maps in your Bible to determine if they are sufficient for your study needs. If not, invest in a separate atlas.

Handbooks: Most handbooks can be found for $15–$20. Again, if you purchase only one Bible study book, the handbook is the one to buy.

Some excellent places to pick up Bible concordances, dictionaries, and other study books are secondhand bookstores, flea markets, antique stores, and book sales. Prices can be as low as a dollar or two for a single-volume dictionary. Computer users should consider purchasing at least one Bible software package. Prices are as low as $30–$40. As in all things, let your intuition and good judgment guide you in purchasing these tools.

Summary

The average English Bible contains around 750,000 words. Bible concordances, dictionaries, commentaries, handbooks, and atlases enable us to get the upper hand on the Bible's words rather than allowing their numbers, complexity, and mysterious nature to overwhelm us. It is to your advantage to avail yourself of these particular Bible study tools.

Notes

1. My 386 computer with a DOS Bible program takes just four seconds to find the instances and verses to a word, regardless of the number.

2. See Chapter 5, Computer Bibles, for a list of Bible software companies.

3. Unity's *Metaphysical Bible Dictionary* and *The Revealing Word* are discussed in Chapter 4.

4. Also see 2 Kings 25:25, 1 Chronicles 8:38—9:44, 2 Chronicles 19:11, 2 Chronicles 23:1, and Ezra 10:22.

5. F. N. Peloubet and Alice D. Adams (eds.), *Peloubet's Bible Dictionary* (Philadelphia: The John C. Winston Company, 1947), p. 278.

6. They also publish two of the best Bible dictionaries (see Bible dictionaries). Abingdon has just come out with *The New Interpreter's Bible* using the NIV and NRSV Bibles.

7. George Arthur Buttrick et al. (eds.), *The Interpreter's Bible, Volume VI* (Nashville: Abingdon, 1982), p. 266.

8. Ibid., pp. 266–67.

9. Ibid., p. 270.

10. Ibid., pp. 270–71.

11. Ibid., pp. 254–55.

12. John 4:5 mentions Sychar as the location of Jacob's plot of land. Could this be the ancient city of Shechem? Perhaps Shechem became Sychar.

13. According to the Jewish historian, Josephus, Vespasian passed through Shechem during a military campaign. *Works of Josephus,* War, IV, viii, 1.

14. In this analogy of tools, a Bible handbook is likened to a pair of vise grips. This tool, rather than designed for a singular use (i.e., screwdriver), performs a variety of functions.

15. My son Nathan is particularly interested in dinosaur books based on the Bible. The pictures are great, however the commentary can be a bit unusual, since dinosaurs were not a part of the biblical landscape.

Chapter 7

Close to the Source

Most of us have seen at least one James Bond movie. These fictional accounts about the life of secret agent 007, based on Ian Fleming's books, rank as one of the most successful movie series in history. When 007 is racing down the road at 100 miles per hour, we are right there beside him in his specially equipped Aston Martin pushing the buttons that fire the hidden missiles at his assailants. If someone casually asks him his name, the next words to slip from our tongues are "the name is Bond, James Bond." Somehow we instinctively know that 007 prefers his vodka martini shaken, not stirred. Either we personally identify with James Bond or we see ourselves as his most-trusted companion.

The producers of the James Bond movies have created films that are entertaining, interesting, and seemingly realistic. Yet do they accurately depict the life of a government spy? Probably not. Nonfiction books about the lives of actual secret agents can be helpful in gaining some knowledge about the spy business. However, the best way to find out what really goes on, short of becoming an agent ourselves, is to get closer to the source. A visit to CIA headquarters or an interview with a working agent may help us to discern the difference between the everyday reality of a secret agent and the fantasy world of James Bond. So, you may wonder, what does James Bond have to do with reading the Bible?[1]

Consider the quest for spiritual knowledge. Mature spiritual aspirants seek the most authentic sources of information and instruction. We want to read and listen to those who, through their own efforts, have touched and embraced the heights of divine consciousness. These teachers speak directly from their own experience and understanding and not from anyone else's books, notes, or courses. Their words are powerful and influential because they come straight from the source of Truth expressing in and through them.

There are others who write about spiritual teachers. Their books can be interesting and informative. However, many of these authors express a limited awareness of their subject's ideas. Their understanding of spirituality is often secondhand, filtered or *translated* through the tool of their intellect. Because of this circumstance, the distance from the reader to the source of Truth is lengthened. How does this line of reasoning relate to the Bible?

The biggest challenge facing Bible students is the simple fact that our Bibles are translations. Any translation, no matter how well done, creates distance between the original author and the modern-day reader. This book has placed considerable attention and importance upon Bible translation. Why? Because, translation is integral to the interpretive process. We have already seen how translations of the same passage can differ depending on whose Bible you are reading. Although this scholastic nitpicking may not greatly affect one's understanding of the basic story line, it can significantly impact one's interpretation of specific words and phrases.

> **"Your faith has made you well."**
> —Mark 5:34

Which begs the question, whose translation is the most accurate and precise? Unfortunately, there is no exact way of knowing. We tend to gravitate toward those translations we find easiest to read. Yet is there a way to transcend biblical translation and reveal the original intent of the biblical writers?

Can the average Bible student get closer to the source of the Bible's words? Is it possible to shorten the distance to biblical truth? Fortunately, the answer is yes.

It is possible to bypass the filter of biblical translation and more deeply apprehend the words of the Bible. However, there is a price to pay. You must be willing to enlist as an operative in the BSS, the Biblical Secret Service.[2] To become a scriptural secret agent is not for the biblically faint of heart but for the more adventuresome Bible student. A knowledge of foreign languages, especially Hebrew and Greek, is helpful but not required. Although a Walther PPK[3] will not be issued, other specialized devices and implements such as lexicons, parallel Bibles, and that old and trustworthy blunderbuss, *Strong's Exhaustive Concordance,* will enable you to complete your mission. You are now about to enter the hidden, inside, secret world of biblical espionage!

WARNING! IMPORTANT NOTICE! THE REMAINDER OF THIS CHAPTER IS CLASSIFIED TOP SECRET AND IS ONLY TO BE READ BY AGENTS OF THE BIBLICAL SECRET SERVICE!

If you are reading this paragraph, then you bought the enlistment propaganda of the previous pages. Good! Welcome aboard! You are hereby officially an agent of the BSS. You may be wondering what awaits you during your service with the agency. Will you become fluent in ancient Hebrew and Greek by the end of the chapter? Will you toss aside your NRSV in favor of reading the ancient manuscripts? Will you amaze your friends by reciting the Lord's Prayer just as Jesus originally did? The answer to all three questions: No.

Reading the rest of this chapter will not improve your fluency in any other language except perhaps English. As with all foreign languages, it takes years of study and practice to be able to speak and/or read ancient Hebrew and Greek with any degree of expertise, which also means that you better hang on to that new NRSV study Bible you recently bought. What did it cost you . . . about forty bucks? As far as speaking like Jesus, well, even if you were versed in New Testament Greek, you would be at a loss to imitate Jesus' Galilean dialect of Aramaic.[4]

What you will learn is how to investigate the various definitions of individual Hebrew and Greek words through a process biblical scholars call "exegesis."[5] If you desire to know alternative meanings to a word or phrase in your English Bible, the tools presented in this chapter will help you uncover these. By the time you have worked a few missions as a BSS agent, you will see the value of this form of scriptural espionage, especially when doing interpretation. Now it's off to biblical secret agent school!

Biblical Languages and Manuscripts

The languages of the Bible, Hebrew and Greek, are among the most ancient in existence. The beginnings of these languages can be traced back over three millennia, and yet they are still in use today by people on the soil where they originated. Bear in mind, languages change over time. The Attic Greek of Plato differs in sound, style, and content from modern Greek. Consider how strange the Elizabethan English of William Shakespeare would sound to a late twentieth-century American speaker.

Similar differences in language content and style exist between biblical books, even those written in the same language. This is due to the variations in language that occurred over the time the books were written as well as the multitudinous nature of biblical authorship. For example, the author of Luke and Acts uses a Greek that is far more refined than the awkward and crude lingo of the author of Revelation. These distinctive writing styles bleed through their English translations. Read a couple of chapters from each book. In your opinion, which books are the easiest to read? The most difficult?

There are no original biblical manuscripts. They are long gone. There are copies of copies of copies of the original manuscripts. As in the composition of the Bible (discussed in Chapter 2), this copying procedure has had its human element. Scribes made simple copying mistakes as well as edited the grammar and words when they felt they could improve upon the text. It's a lot like the telephone game. A message is passed around a circle of people until it returns to the beginning. The final message usually does not resemble its original. The results of this centuries-old process are numerous manuscripts that differ slightly in content. When we read the Hebrew Old Testament or the Greek New Testament, we are reading the best scholarly compilation of the manuscript copies presently available.

This situation brings up some interesting questions regarding the integrity of the scriptures. From a scientific point of view, the Bible is about as imperfect, imprecise, and convoluted a document as can be found. Although the Bible contains principles, ideas and laws that can be scientifically demonstrated, it is not a scientific writing. Its integrity and validity are matters of faith. The fact that the Bible speaks to so many people at a deep spiritual level is testimony to its potency and character. In spite of all the human hands that have fashioned, altered, and corrupted the manuscripts and their subsequent copies, the Bible endures. It is as if the Bible has had a guardian angel or two protecting and nurturing its evolution. The current finished product is one that continues to inspire its readers.

> **"Give, and it will be given to you. A good measure, pressed down, shaken together, running over, will be put into your lap; for the measure you give will be the measure you get back."**
>
> —Luke 6:38

Back to the languages of the Bible. Ancient Hebrew and

Greek are the principal languages of the biblical manuscripts.[6] Although both languages have distinctly different roots, they have coexisted in the history and composition of the Bible over the centuries.

Hebrew is a Semitic language, as is Aramaic, Arabic, and ancient Akkadian and Canaanite. It is written from right to left and originally had only consonants. For instance, David reads as דוד, or DVD. Vowels and other marks were added during the Middle Ages by the Masoretes[7] to aid in pronunciation and grammar. The Masoretic Text (MT), on which most translations of the Old Testament are based, was the only known Old Testament manuscript until the discovery of the Dead Sea Scrolls. The oldest MT manuscripts date to the tenth–eleventh century C.E.

During the fourth century B.C.E., the Macedonian general, Alexander the Great, conquered the lands of the Middle East including Palestine. For centuries thereafter, Greek came into common use by people throughout the ancient world. After his conquest of Egypt in 331 B.C.E., Alexander founded the city of Alexandria, which bears his name. Many Jews immigrated to Alexandria and formed a distinct community within the city. Although they maintained their Jewish religious identity, Greek culture and language entered into their lifestyle. Many Alexandrian Jews eventually lost their ability to express themselves in their native Hebrew.[8] Think of how many second-generation Americans who, through lack of use, abandon the language of their parents.

> **"Very truly, I tell you, the one who believes in me will also do the works that I do and, in fact, will do greater works than these."**
> —John 14:12

This inability to understand Hebrew probably led to the first translation of the Old Testament known today as the Septuagint. Its name is derived from the legend surrounding its creation. According to the legend, Ptolemy II (285–246 B.C.E.), the king of Egypt, requested that a Greek copy of the Hebrew scriptures be produced for inclusion in the library at Alexandria. Supposedly, seventy-two scholars spent seventy-two days completing the translation; hence, the name *Septuagint*, meaning seventy. LXX, the Roman numeral for seventy, is often used by scholars to refer to the Septuagint.

The Septuagint is an important biblical document because (1) it was the earliest translation of the Old Testament used by Greek-speaking Jews, (2) it was the version of the Old Testament quoted by New Testament authors, (3) it was the Old Testament translation of early Greek-speaking Christians, (4) copies of it were found among the Dead Sea Scrolls dating to the second century B.C.E., (5) most books of the Apocrypha come from it, (6) it is more than a thousand years older than the Masoretic Text; many Bible translators consult it for alternative renderings, and (7) it is a natural bridge between the Old and New Testaments.

Greek, unlike the Semitic Hebrew, is a member of the Indo-European family of languages, as are English and most European languages. It is written from left to right and uses its own alphabet. For instance, David is written as Δαυίδ. You probably recognized the first letter of David as the uppercase *delta*, Δ. The lowercase letters of Greek are generally less familiar to most people.

Greek also makes use of accent marks in pronunciation, such as the mark above the ί. To achieve the English *H* sound, Greek uses breathing marks in front of vowels. The *hay* sound is written as ‛H whereas *ay* is spelled as ’H. A little squiggle (’) makes a difference in pronunciation. Don't be too confused by the H. It is the Greek letter *eta* and is pronounced with a long *a* sound.

Thousands of copies of the Greek New Testament have been produced over the centuries, many differing in content. *The Interpreter's Dictionary of the Bible* states "the text of the NT contains more variants than that of any other body of ancient literature."[9] One of the earliest Greek New Testaments was published by the sixteenth-century Dutch scholar Erasmus. His

Greek New Testament became the source material for Tyndale's English translation. Today's versions are produced by an extremely tedious analysis of material from hundreds of sources, resulting in a usable, believable document. Many Greek New Testaments cite each of these sources throughout their text.

The Hebrew Masoretic Text, Greek Septuagint, and Greek New Testaments comprise the main sources of material for the Bible. Their published forms were as close to the source of their author's words as anyone could reach, that is, until the discovery of the Dead Sea Scrolls.

Dead Sea Scrolls

Any discussion of biblical manuscripts must include the Dead Sea Scrolls. Considerable importance has been placed upon these documents since their discovery nearly fifty years ago. Who wrote them? Where did they come from? What makes them so special?

In 1947 a group of Bedouins ventured into the hills northwest of the Dead Sea into an area called Qumran. While searching for a lost animal, they discovered a cave that contained jars housing ancient leather scrolls. Many of these scrolls were taken to a merchant in Bethlehem. Eventually, the scrolls ended up in the hands of scholars who were able to date them to the second century B.C.E. Among these scrolls was a complete book of Isaiah. Following the Arab-Israeli war of 1947–49, excavations at other caves in the vicinity of Qumran produced hundreds of additional scrolls.

Near the caves are the ruins of the walled community known as Khirbet Qumran. Analysis of these ruins has led scholars to attribute the scrolls to the former inhabitants of the Qumran community. Many scholars believe the inhabitants to have been members of the Jewish Essene sect, mentioned in the writings of the Roman scholar Pliny and the Jewish historian Josephus. The scrolls and fragments represent the library of the Essenes, stored in the caves for posterity or safety. The scrolls consist of (1) complete copies or fragments of nearly every book of the Hebrew Bible, (2) Apocryphal and non-canonical writings, (3) scriptural commentaries, and (4) sectarian writings for use by the community.

So, why are the Dead Sea Scrolls so important? Because they are older than any biblical manuscripts known prior to their discovery. In the world of manuscripts, older is better. In fact, the Dead Sea Scrolls are over a thousand years older than the oldest known Masoretic text!

From a practical point of view, the Dead Sea Scrolls have enabled modern Bible translators to confirm the accuracy of the manuscripts already in use as well as offer alternative meanings. They have also given historians a glimpse into the life and mind of the ancient Essenes. Their discovery has placed humanity an entire millennium closer to the source of the Bible's original words.

Using Hebrew and Greek to Interpret the Bible

Now that you have been briefed on the background of Biblical Secret Service manuscripts and languages, it's time for you to begin your first mission. You will require two tools: (1) KJV Bible and (2) *Strong's Exhaustive Concordance of the Bible.* Optional equipment includes a Hebrew-Chaldee lexicon of the Old Testament and a Greek-English lexicon of the New Testament. Your mission: Examine the meanings of the words *shepherd* in the 23rd Psalm and *hallowed* in the Lord's Prayer.

Let's begin with the Old Testament. The text of the KJV of Psalm 23 reads, "The Lord is my shepherd; I shall not want." Look up *shepherd* in the main concordance of Strong's. The line should read:

"Ps 23:1 The Lord is my *s* I shall not want." [10]

The *s* represents the word *shepherd* in the verse. Next, look up the number above the " mark. It's just a few lines above. The number is 7462. Go to the Hebrew-Chaldee Dictionary toward the back of the book. Look up 7462. Presto! You are now in contact with the Hebrew word for *shepherd.* The text reads:

> 7462. רָעָה **ra'ah,** *raw-ah:* a prim. root: to *tend* a flock, i.e. *pasture* it; intrans. to *graze* (lit. or fig.); gen. to *rule;* by extens. to *associate* with (as a friend):—x break, companion, keep company with, devour, eat up evil entreat, feed, use as a friend, make friendship with herdman, keep [sheep] (-er), pastor, + shearing house, shepherd, wander, waste.[11]

Notice the number of meanings רָעָה has. It means "pasture," "graze," "rule," "associate," and so on. Here's where the fun begins. Using these additional meanings, consider new renderings for Psalm 23. Focus on words related to shepherd. For instance, "The Lord is my companion; I shall not want." Or how about, "The Lord is my friend, I shall not want"? Play around with the phraseology a little. The basic meaning of the verse denotes God's presence in our lives. We might interpret the passage: "God *rules* my life, I have no wants"; or "God *tends* to my needs; therefore, I do not want for anything."

Let's move on to the New Testament. The beginning of the Lord's Prayer according to the KJV of Matthew 6:9 reads, *"Our Father which art in heaven, Hallowed be thy name."* Our word is *hallowed.* The main concordance lists it:

"M't 6:9 in heaven, *H·* be thy name." The number 37 is given.[12]

Look up 37 in the Greek New Testament Dictionary located in the back, right after the Hebrew-Chaldee Dictionary. Way to go! You are now face-to-face with the Greek word for *hallowed.* The text reads:

"37. ἁγιάζω **hagiazo**, *hag-ee-ad'-zo;* from *40;* to *make holy,* i.e. (cer.) *purify* or *consecrate;* (mentally) to *venerate:*—hallow, be holy, sanctify."[13]

Begin by trying some different renderings of the verse. Consider: "Our Father which art in heaven, your name is purified," and, "Our Father which art in heaven, venerated is your name." Also the definition refers readers to listing 40. Look up 40 as well as other related words (38, 39, 41, and 42) for additional ideas. Again, as with the Old Testament, do some creative thinking about the passage. It is the opening words of the most famous prayer in the world. Prayer is done to transform one's consciousness. We could interpret the passage this way: The use of God's name in prayer makes my heart and mind pure, holy, and consecrated.

This very process of biblical word study can be speeded up dramatically by using every secret agent's friend, the computer. Bible computer programs not only contain English translations but Hebrew and Greek texts and dictionaries. In a matter of seconds, you can call up the Bible's original words in their transliterated[14] forms along with their definitions from Strong's dictionaries. There are some programs that allow the computer screen to be split into various sections showing the English text, the Hebrew and Greek transliteration, and Strong's dictionary definitions all at once!

Another step you can take in discovering the meaning of the Hebrew and Greek words is to consult a special dictionary or lexicon. These books go into greater detail than Strong's in explaining the use of words in the Bible and in other literature. They can be a gold mine of ideas that lead to new interpretations.

The ultimate step a Bible student can take is to learn to read ancient Hebrew and Greek. I have done both. You can learn these languages by taking courses from universities, colleges, and traditional seminaries as well as by reading books on the subject. Some Christian bookstores sell Hebrew Old Testaments, Greek New Testaments, and their respective lexicons. Polyglot (multiple translation) versions are available, showing English alongside the original languages. Hebrew and Greek tutorial programs are also available for computers.

From experience, Greek is easier to learn. The reason is that Hebrew's Semitic nature provides few if any related words in English. Hebrew uses an alphabet that looks nothing like English and is written from right to left. In spite of these obstacles, Hebrew is worth learning if you have enough desire.

As mentioned earlier, Greek and English are members of the Indo-European language family. Much of the English language is derived from Greek. Although the Greek alphabet differs from the English, there are some similarities, and it becomes more familiar with use. Unlike Hebrew, Greek is written from the more conventional left to right.

There is nothing quite as exhilarating as actually reading the text of the Bible in its original language. My college Greek professor made me orally translate the entire book of Philemon for my final exam. Thankfully, the book of Philemon is only twenty-five verses long and is written in the relatively easy-to-read conversational Greek of Paul. I passed the exam. I don't know if I would pass today. As with all languages, consistent use leads to proficiency. What I have found is that familiarity with Hebrew and Greek is very helpful in using the *Strong's Concordance*, reading the lexicons, and occasionally scanning the text.

> **"For 'In him we live and move and have our being'; as even some of your own poets have said, 'For we too are his offspring.'"**
> —Acts 17:28

Summary

Congratulations! You have completed your first mission for the BSS. Was it as hard as you thought it would be? How do you think James Bond would have done? Future missions are a matter between you and the Admiralty of the Bible within. Hopefully, you are beginning to see the merit of this kind of biblical investigation. It is a tool that frees you from being completely at the mercy of biblical translations and gives you more options in determining your interpretations of scripture.

The experience of spirituality comes from consciously moving our individual awareness closer to the indwelling Presence. The closer we advance, the more authentic and clearer are our experiences. Much the same can be said of Bible study. As you examine the Bible in its original languages, you will be a bit more in touch with the meaning and message of its authors than if you only read translations. You will be closer to the source.

Notes

1. Read Joshua 2:1–24 for a story about some ancient secret agents.

2. Not to be confused with the British Secret Service.

3. James Bond's handgun.

4. Although the authors of The Gospels wrote in Greek, Jesus' language was Aramaic. We can be reasonably certain that all of Jesus' words were translated from Aramaic into Greek before being written down in the manuscripts.

5. Pronounced, ex-uh-jee-sus.

6. A few phrases of the Old Testament were written in Aramaic. See footnote #8, Chapter 5.

7. The term assigned to those Jewish scholars and scribes who preserved the text of the Hebrew Bible for hundreds of years of the early common era. Their name is derived from the word *masorah,* meaning tradition.

8. By 300 B.C.E., Aramaic was becoming the language of Palestine, replacing Hebrew. Its predominance continued well into the Common Era. Syriac, a later form of Aramaic, is spoken today by Christians living in Kurdistan (N. Iraq.)

9. George Arthur Buttrick et al. (eds.), *The Interpreter's Dictionary of the Bible, R-Z* (Nashville: Abingdon, 1982), p. 612.

10. James Strong, *Strong's Exhaustive Concordance of the Bible*, p. 917.

11. James Strong, *A Concise Dictionary of the Words in The Hebrew Bible*, p. 109.

12. James Strong, *Strong's Exhaustive Concordance of the Bible*, p. 433.

13. James Strong, *A Concise Dictionary of the Words in The Greek New Testament*, p. 7.

14. The Hebrew and Greek words are written using their approximate English (Latin) letters. For instance, the Greek ἀγγελος becomes *aggelos*, meaning angel (note—in Greek, two g's together make an *ng* sound).

Part III.

Interpreting the Bible for Spiritual Growth

Chapter 8

Everyone Interprets the Bible

Have you come across someone who said to you, "I don't go in for this interpretation stuff, I just take the Bible literally"? If you have, don't believe them for an instant. Why? Because, no one can read the Bible without interpreting it in some way. Do we always see life in a strictly straight-ahead, prosaic, word-for-word manner, uninfluenced by the ideas of others, void of any personal interpretation? Hardly. Given the multidimensional nature of human beings, it is nonsensical to suggest that a singular explanation of life is possible for all people. We all put our own unique spin on life's meaning and alter that spin throughout our lives. There are as many views of life as there are people. The same rationale holds true for the Bible. We all interpret the Bible using our own individual frames of reference, our own self-styled rose-colored glasses. Indeed, it is our interpretations that make the Bible come alive and have meaning for us.

Moreover, the Bible is simply too complex a document to be *taken literally*. It exhibits infinite shades of gray. In fact, a literal interpretation is logically impossible, given the number of contradictions the Bible presents (see Chapter 2). How do we account, for example, for the different versions of Saul's death? In 1 Samuel 31:4, we read that Saul committed suicide by falling on his sword. In 2 Samuel 1:9–10, we learn that an Amalekite killed Saul. Speaking of death, who really killed Goliath? David, you say. Maybe, and then again, maybe not. 1 Samuel 17:50 states that David killed Goliath, as you probably thought. Ah, but in 2 Samuel 21:19, we read that Elhanan killed Goliath. So, who killed Goliath?

This type of scriptural duplicity sends the biblical literalists into an intellectual no-man's-land from which there is no rational escape. Of course logic is not especially high on the agenda of the Bible literalists. To them, the Bible has no incongruities or peculiarities. Even though the Bible asserts that David as well as Elhanan killed Goliath, Bible literalists, blinded by their own self-induced narrowness, cannot see the two differing accounts. David killed Goliath, and that's the end of that subject. The only escape from the box of biblical literalism is the willingness to look for explanations and reasons for these discrepancies beyond the words on the page. That is, we must be willing to interpret scripture.

Most of us have had the pleasure of shopping for a car. You've read *Consumer's Reports,* talked to the experts, and know exactly what kind of car you want to buy. For discussion's sake, let's say you want a red Studebaker.[1] You can see it in your mind's eye—bright, shiny, beautiful. You search the dealers, looking for that perfect car. For the next couple of weeks, all you see on the road are red Studebakers. They seem to be everywhere. You wonder if this is a sign from God that you are destined to buy one. Is this a sign from God? Not necessarily. What you are experiencing is selective perception, looking at life through the lens of a red Studebaker. The red Studebakers were there all the time unnoticed by you before. The mental image of the red Studebaker drew into your view the object of your desire.

> **"Do not be conformed to this world, but be transformed by the renewing of your minds, so that you may discern what is the will of God—what is good and acceptable and perfect."**
>
> —Romans 12:2

What does buying a car have to do with interpreting the Bible? Like the automotive customer, we tend to only see in the Bible what our lenses of perception allow. The more dogmatic our perception, the less we are able to grasp. Our states of consciousness directly determine our biblical interpretations. If we are looking for passages that encourage living an abundant life, we will find them. If we are looking for references that support the virtues of being poor and destitute, they will show themselves to us. We will find in the Bible what we want to find. If we want to find something new, we must change our lenses of interpretation. This chapter illustrates nine lenses through which we interpret the Bible and life in general. The nine interpretative lenses are these: factual, historical, dramatic, comedic, literary, moral, allegorical, prophetic, and metaphysical.

Factual

Perhaps you have seen an episode of the old television show *Dragnet*. The star of the show, Sergeant Joe Friday, often used the phrase, *"just the facts, ma'am,"* when questioning a female witness to a crime. When we interpret the Bible factually, and I use the word *factually* very loosely, we are attempting to determine if what we are reading actually happened. The factual level of interpretation is as close to a literal reading of the Bible as we can come.

The events in the Bible happened so long ago that the facts have had a long time to become skewed. Indeed, there are honest facts presented in the Bible but few we can trust with 100 percent certainty. Unlike Sergeant Joe Friday, we have no witnesses to question, no signed depositions, no judges reviewing the case. In matters of law, if something happens, we usually like some kind of evidence to back up the story. As Bible students, the only evidence we have at our disposal is archaeology, the biblical manuscripts themselves, and the writings of other authors from the biblical era.[2] Therefore, Bible facts are primarily judgment calls. On the basis of the information at hand, we make our best intelligent guess whether a story is factual or not. We might better describe this process as assessing the *probable* facts.

For example: We could safely say that the writer of John was accurate in documenting that *Jesus wept* at the tomb of Lazarus.[3] After all, it is natural for someone to cry at the grave of a deceased loved one. There is little reason for the writer to lie about Jesus' expression of grief. In all probability, Jesus cried for his friend. It is a probable fact.

In the book of Exodus we read, "Bezalel made the ark of acacia wood; it was two and a half cubits long, a cubit and a half wide, and a cubit and a half high."[4] It is hard to argue with these dimensions for the Ark of the Covenant. Even though there are no eye witnesses or other documentation to support this statement, we can reasonably accept that it was built to these specifications. Again, it is a probable fact.

Historical

History is the presentation of factual accounts of human experiences. We depend upon our history books to tell us the truth. Many look to the Bible as a history book of ancient times. Although it does serve that purpose, it does so imperfectly. How so, you may wonder?

The Bible was not written as a history book in the modern sense of the word. Modern history books must pass some level of professional and scientific scrutiny. Their purpose is to be accurate. The biblical writers had no such intent. They wrote history, but with the aim of promoting a certain religious viewpoint. They wrote a biased history. As a result, many stories were apparently exaggerated for religious purposes.

For example: In the book of Joshua, we read about the exploits of the Israelite army in eradicating the Canaanites from the land, only to have the Canaanites return with a vengeance in the book of Judges. Were all the Canaanites wiped out during Joshua's leadership or not? Apparently not. However, it makes for a much better story to have the hero-leader Joshua be completely triumphant in securing the Promised Land for the Israelite people. The likely story is that his conquest of Canaan was only partial.

Back to David's slaying of Goliath. As we have already discovered, the stories in 1 Samuel and 2 Samuel conflict with each other. There is no way of knowing for certain who killed Goliath. However, it sounds much better to have David, the famous king, defeat the formidable Goliath rather than some commoner like Elhanan. Interestingly, the writer of Chronicles, who wrote about 200 years

"For we are the temple of the living God."
—2 Corinthians 6:16

after 1 and 2 Samuel, attempted to rewrite the story in favor of David by saying: "Again there was war with the Philistines; and Elhanan son of Jair killed Lahmi the brother of Goliath the Gittite, the shaft of whose spear was like a weaver's beam."[5] Elhanan now becomes the victor over Lahmi, Goliath's brother, thus preserving David's place in *history* as the man who slew Goliath with a simple slingshot.

The Bible, therefore, is a pseudohistorical book. There is history in the Bible. Much of what we learn about the ancient world comes from the Bible. However, we must always keep in mind the intent of the biblical writers. They wrote not to perfectly preserve the events of the past but to tell the epic story of God's chosen people and how God worked through them to bring it all about. They wrote to instill in their readers and listeners a sense of importance and magnificence regarding their spiritual origins. Along the way, these writers took some literary license in telling their tales. When was the last time you told a fish story? How big was that one that got away? Uh-huh! Bible commentaries and study notes can be very useful when determining the historicity of a Bible story.

Dramatic

Jacob marries Leah while in love with her sister Rachel—father-in-law, Laban, suspected in bride swapping![6]

JUDAH SLEEPS WITH PROSTITUTE WHO TURNS OUT TO BE HIS DAUGHTER-IN-LAW![7]

Samson falls for Delilah who cuts off his hair while he sleeps![8]

David arranges Uriah's death to pursue his wife Bathsheba![9]

The scene turns ugly when Jesus confronts angry lynch mob![10]

Judas betrays Jesus to Caiaphas for money![11]

Freak earthquake damages prison, jailer distraught and nearly kills self; Paul and Silas finally pardoned by the magistrate![12]

Are these the headlines of a checkout stand tabloid or the cover of the *Soap Opera Digest?* No, these are actual listings of episodes from the hit TV show *As the Bible Turns.*

Bible characters and their stories make for excellent soap opera. In a way, the books of Samuel and Kings read like such good soap scripts that they could almost be renamed *As the Kingdoms Turn.* We read of Saul's insane jealousy of David, David's dirty little business with Bathsheba, Solomon's hundreds of foreign wives, Jeroboam splitting off the house of David, Baal worship, treacherous plots against one another, everybody doing "evil in the sight of the Lord."[13] This material is the stuff of which soaps are made!

The Bible accurately depicts the human condition. Yet we so highly exalt Bible characters in our minds that we can easily forget that they were real people with very human problems, foibles, and reactions. These were not merely characters in a Cecil B. De Mille[14] film, but were flesh and blood people with many of the same problems we have today. Their humanity is often what makes them approachable, touchable, and not all that unlike ourselves.

To interpret the Bible from the dramatic level requires that we get in touch with our own humanity. Read the stories as if you were watching characters on a stage or screen. Put yourself in their places. How do these characters and their stories grab you? Do you find yourself especially relating to any of them? How so? Have you ever been in a similar predicament? Explore your own reactions to their circumstances. Use your imagination. For a moment, consider Jesus' healing of the epileptic boy from Mark 9:17–29.[15] Imagine you are the father of the boy:

My son has been afflicted with this mysterious disease since birth, one that has nearly taken his life on several occasions. I have long anguished over his condition and have felt completely helpless to do anything about it. From one moment to the next, I live in fearful anticipation of my son's death. Everyone in town says he is possessed by demons. My love for him tells me to ignore these diagnoses, but in my weaker moments, I wonder if they may be right.

> **"The fruit of the Spirit is love, joy, peace, patience, kindness, generosity, faithfulness, gentleness, and self-control."**
> —Galatians 5:22–23

Look! There is Jesus. I have heard incredible stories about him. Perhaps he can heal him. I shall bring my son to Jesus and ask for his help. Jesus replies, "If you are able!—All things can be done for the one who believes" (Mk. 9:23). I am petrified. Did I say something wrong? What, me believe? I have run out of belief. My heart cries, "heal my child," but the next words from my mouth plead, "I believe; help my unbelief!" (Mk. 9:24). Before I can say another word, my son is healed, completely. I am exhausted, yet overjoyed. For the first time in our lives, I hold my son in my arms without a single pang of anxiety.

The original biblical story has a factual dimension to it. It reads like an eyewitness account. Given that it is genuine, the boy and his father were actual people whom Jesus encountered during his ministry. My expansion of the original story presents a likely scenario of the father's internal experience. In writing it, I simply projected myself into the father's psyche and began asking some basic questions: What has life been like with such a son as this? What are my true feelings about him? In my interaction with Jesus, how am I apt to respond? How do I feel now that my son is healed? Empathizing with the father, I let my answers flow forth onto the page.

The stories in the Bible have all the drama and emotion of a television screenplay. They are also about real people who had the good fortune of having details of their lives written down for us to read thousands of years later. If you are looking for drama, the Bible has it. The footnotes of the previously mentioned headlines will guide you to a few good stories. There are countless others. Through the dramatic interpretive lens, you can always tune in to another episode of *As the Bible Turns.*

Comedic

The Bible usually does not top the list of those books we read for comic relief. To many Christians, it may seem irreverent to look for humor in the Bible. Humor is a tricky thing and is a matter of personal taste. We don't always find amusing what others do, and vice versa. It is highly unlikely that the biblical writers intended their stories to be funny.

> **"For by grace you have been saved through faith, and this is not your own doing; it is the gift of God."**
> —Ephesians 2:8

However, if you are willing to look with an eye for humor, the Bible can provide just as much material for situation comedies as it does soap operas.

The Bible's people make it comical. As in the case of the dramatic, the comedic interpretive lens calls for us to see Bible characters as real-life people and, in the same breath, examine our own humanness. The essential difference between the two interpretive approaches is that the comedic twists the stories just a wee bit to derive humor from them. As with most modern-day comedians, we must hunt for the simplest aspects of a story and amplify them in a humorous direction.

If you are having trouble doing this, spend some time watching the opening monologue by the host from one of the late-night talk shows, such as the *Tonight Show* with Jay Leno or *Late Night* with David Letterman. If you go to bed early, set your VCR to record the shows for viewing at another time. You will notice that these comedians take everyday news events and tell them back to their audiences with a humorous bent. Most of the time they succeed, and the audience laughs and applauds. Occasionally their jokes flop, and they go on to the next one. As I mentioned earlier, humor is a tricky business. Using the same method, you can uncover the humor in scripture. Ultimately, you must determine what is funny to you.[16]

Here is a story I have found to be amusing. Open your Bible and turn to Exodus 3:1—4:17. In this scene, Moses is standing before the burning bush receiving his call to free the Israelites from their bondage to the Egyptians. Here is how we might retell the story in a comedic manner:

God: Moses, I want you to go and talk to the Pharaoh about freeing My people.

Moses: Who me? You've got to be kidding. You are kidding, aren't You?

God: Not at all, my friend. I'll be with you. Don't you worry.

Moses: You know, God, the people aren't going to believe me when I tell them that I'm going to get them freed. And, You know, they're going to want to know what Your name is. Telling them that their ancestor's God has been talking to me just isn't going to cut it with them.

God: Just tell them My name is I AM WHO I AM, but that's not important right now. Get busy, Moses—there's lots of work to be done! These Egyptians have been bad news for My people. Boy, I'm sure going to show those guys a few things. Start getting everybody ready for a road trip.

Moses: Yeah, but what if they won't believe me, or even listen to me? What if they tell me I've been smoking something? They're gonna think that I've gone off the deep end!

God: For crying out loud, Moses, where's your faith, man? You're such a wimp. I can't believe My own judgment in picking you for this job. Of course, who's to say that another human would do any better. Okay, hold on a minute. What's that in your hand?

Moses: Um, it's a rod.

God: Well, toss it on the ground. Oh, be sure to step back a bit. These miracles sometimes require a bit of elbow room. (The rod becomes a snake. Moses is scared of snakes.)

Moses: Ahhhh! (Moses takes off running.)

God: Hey, Moses, get on back here, you chicken! That's just a little garter snake. What did you think I was going to do, turn the rod into a cobra or rattlesnake? I need you alive to carry out this mission. Go on, now, pick up the snake. It won't bite. I promise. (Moses comes back and gingerly picks up the snake. It instantly turns back into a rod.)

Moses: Don't scare me like that, God. Your Omnipotence knows that I'm afraid of snakes.

God: You better get over that snake phobia, Moses. You're gonna do that trick a few times before this thing is over. Now, touch your chest. Go ahead. It won't hurt. (Moses touches his chest, and it immediately becomes covered with a white, scaly substance—leprosy.)

Moses: Yuk—gross! What is this stuff? Get it off me! Get it off me!

God: Relax, Moses. Just put your hand back on your chest. (The leprosy disappears.) They'll believe you now. Even David Copperfield can't top this magic. Well, if they don't go for those two, I've got some ideas about turning the river into blood. That'll scare the pants off them, especially so close to Halloween, don't you think?

Moses: All right, God, those are some pretty hot tricks.

However, I've got to tell You something. I got a D– in high school speech class. Even my wife Zipporah leads the table blessings because I choke so badly when doing public speaking. You know the people won't listen to me if I'm not a good speaker. (Moses thinks he's got God stumped.)

God: (Shaking His head.) I've failed. I create humankind after My own image and likeness, and they act like such idiots! (To Moses.) Hey, Moses, who made you? Me. That's right, Me. And, if I made you, then you're going to be able to handle this little project of mine just fine. Is that clear? Now get out of here, go, and I'll tell you what to say.

Moses: (On his knees.) Oh, please, God, send someone else! I don't want to go.

God: Moses, you're really starting to tick Me off. (The burning bush blazes a bit more brightly.) Now, how about your brother Aaron? His school records indicate that he got a B+ in speech class. That's good enough for Me. Here's how we'll do it. I'll give you the words and then you can tell Aaron what to say. Is it a deal or what? Oh, look, here he comes now. Why don't you try out that rod-snake trick on him?

This is an example of how you can take a simple Bible story and fashion it in a funny, entertaining way. In this case, I have exploited Moses' lack of self-confidence for our amusement. Of course we might ask ourselves how we would fare given the same set of circumstances. Perhaps we are simply lampooning our own propensities toward a certain behavior. Be aware, not all characters and stories have comedic potential. You'll have to experiment with this interpretive lens a bit until it begins to work for you.

Literary

Chapters 1 and 2 discussed some of the parameters of good writing—namely, relevancy and readability. They also pointed to the Bible as a piece of literature that many modern people consider to be inapplicable to their lifestyle and somewhat laborious to read. These perceptions are valid when compared with most books. Nevertheless, in spite of these hindrances, this book has endeavored to demonstrate the literary relevance of the Bible and to enable the student to read it as one would any other spiritually oriented book.

Along with having good drama and humor, the Bible is also good literature. However, not all writing in the Bible is good literature. Some parts read very easily; others do not. Many passages, as well as entire books, are rather boring to read, resembling technical manuals or legal documents. Generally speaking, the books of Leviticus, Numbers, Deuteronomy, Ezra, and Nehemiah top the boring list.

To read the Bible through the literary lens (not to be confused with literal), we must become discriminating readers. We are looking for good stories, poetry, anything that reads well. Typically, poetry, with its more artistic quality, is more enjoyable to read than prose. These books stand out as some of the best literature in the Bible: Job, Esther, Psalms, Proverbs, Song of Solomon (racy stuff!), Isaiah, Luke, and The Acts of the Apostles.

Our choice of English translation can make a significant difference in the way the Bible reads. (See Chapter 5 for a description of the many English translations available.) The King James Version uses a voice that is old-fashioned, poetic, "Biblespeak." Others use a more contemporary English.

To illustrate this point, let us read a familiar passage using different translations. Many metaphysical Christians are attracted to the phrase from Proverbs 29:18: "Where there is no vision, the people perish" (KJV). Personally interpreted, this idea strongly suggests that having a clear vision for ourselves is necessary to live a worthwhile life. At least this is true according to the King James Version. However, this passage reads much differently according to these particular versions:

RSV: "Where there is no prophecy the people cast off restraint."

Jerusalem: "Where there is no vision the people get out of hand."

New American: "Without prophecy the people become demoralized."

NEB: "Where there is no one in authority, the people break loose."

TEV: "A nation without God's guidance is a nation without order."

NIV: "Where there is no revelation, the people cast off restraint."

CEV: "Without guidance from God law and order disappear."

Jewish Publication Society: "For lack of vision a people lose restraint."

Lamsa: "When the wicked men multiply, the people are ruined."

TLB: "Where there is ignorance of God, the people run wild."

As incredible as it may seem, none of these selections convey exactly the same meaning. None of them agree with the King James Version. You can see that reading the Bible as literature is not as simple as it sounds; it involves some decision making on our part. We must first select the book or passages that we are interested in reading. Second, we must consider which translation(s) to use. Both are a matter of personal preference.

Moral

For centuries countless children have grown up with *Aesop's Fables.* You may recollect these stories from your own childhood, stories such as "The Goose That Laid The Golden Egg," "The Boy Who Cried Wolf," and many others. Attributed to the sixth century B.C.E. storyteller Aesop, these understandable, simple stories have imparted invaluable, moral instructions and virtues to their listeners and readers.

We have all seen cartoons, television shows, or movies where a character's angelic and devilish selves vie with each other for the soul of the individual. On one shoulder, the angelic self suggests an altruistic, unselfish, constructive course of action. On the other shoulder, the devilish self urges a self-seeking, harmful, destructive direction. We commonly call this experience *conscience.* We say, "My conscience would bother me if I cheated on my income tax return," or "I have a clear conscience about the way I handled the negotiations with my employer."

The Bible is, without a doubt, the most referred-to book in the Western world by those seeking or supporting a moral opinion. Many have come to equate the Bible and morality with some conservative religionist's attempts to shove a rigid code of conduct down the throats of any persons in their path (recall the Moral Majority and other like organizations of the 1980s). This moral code is often characterized as Judeo-Christian, yet is strangely applied to all people irrespective of religious background. Unfavorable results await those who do not conform to the edicts of these so-called moral authorities. A person may be labeled either a saint or a scoundrel, depending upon the rules of the appraiser.

> **"Do not worry about anything, but in everything by prayer and supplication with thanksgiving let your requests be made known to God."**
>
> —Philippians 4:6

The real world is not a religiously uniform, homogeneous assemblage. At this point in the history of humanity, diversity rules. Ethical and moral tenets are not always cut-and-dried, but admissible to discussion, exploration, and reaffirmation. As a result, the morality of one person or group may not always agree with that of another. When values are held in common by a group of people, there is peace among the ranks. When one's moral beliefs no longer conform to that of his or her community's, the inevitable result is upset, dissension, and, likely, a parting of the ways. Recently we have seen this clash of moral values played out in the pro-choice/pro-life controversy.

Like it or not, morality has become a matter of interpretation. We must all determine those issues that are of moral importance to us. Ask yourself these questions: What situations trip my conscience meter? What values are dear to me? Do I see myself as being virtuous? What are my personal priorities? Your answers to these questions will indicate to you the nature of your moral outlook, the precepts by which you are living your life.

Despite the great variance of moral viewpoints, most people have a natural, basic sense of morality that transcends denominational, cultural, and generational lines. This morality is composed of those universal spiritual values held in common among the authentic religious traditions of the world (See Chapter 3). Some of these values include courage, forgiveness, honesty, kindness, patience, and many, many others.[17] We instinctively know whether our thoughts, words, and actions are in harmony with or counter to universally held principles. How so, you may ask? Our conscience reminds us.

The Golden Rule is an excellent biblical example of a commonly accepted moral precept: "Do to others as you would have them do to you."[18] This rule embodies many universal spiritual values, especially compassion, kindness, and love. If we expect others to treat us a certain way, we must act in kind. When we behave without regard to the Golden Rule, our conscience nags at us from within until we correct our attitude and behavior.

The moral interpretive lens allows us to delve into the inner world of our own conscience, values, and ideals. Through this lens, we can locate and interpret those Bible verses that reaffirm what we already hold to be morally true for us and/or inspire us to new beliefs. The moral of a passage or story can be explained by asking the questions: What is there to learn? What universal spiritual values are being taught? How can these values work in simplifying the living of my life? How has my life become difficult and challenging when I ignore them? You are looking for the precept behind the words. Begin your study using this interpretive lens with the Ten Commandments, the book of Proverbs, and Jesus' parables.

Allegorical

Allegory is a normal and important element of human thinking and speech. Whenever we attempt to explain the meaning of something symbolically rather than directly, we are using allegory. For instance, "It was raining cats and dogs" is a very simple allegory.[19] Allegories cannot be understood literally, but always imply a meaning other than the obvious. At face value, the above statement implies that cats and dogs actually fell from the sky. However, as an allegory, the cats and dogs symbolize the extreme volume of water that fell as rain. Allegories make language interesting and rich.

The biblical writers made extensive use of allegory in communicating ideas. Many were employed to relate ethical, etiological,[20] and moral teachings to the reader. Jesus' parables are allegorical, full of symbolic characters and objects, each having a greater scope beyond the surface story. Consider the Parable of the Lost Sheep:

> "So he told them this parable: 'Which one of you, having a hundred sheep and losing one of them, does not leave the ninety-nine in the wilderness and go after the one that is lost until he finds it? When he has found it, he lays it on his shoulders and rejoices. And when he comes home, he calls together his friends and neighbors, saying to them, "Rejoice with

me, for I have found my sheep that was lost." Just so,
I tell you, there will be more joy in heaven over one
sinner who repents than over ninety-nine righteous
persons who need no repentance.'"[21]

This story is not about sheep. It's about the importance of
reaching out to all people with a message of spiritual transformation, especially to those who have not experienced it. The
ninety-nine sheep are symbolic of the many people who already possess spiritual understanding. They require less attention than the lost sheep (human soul) whose needs are more
considerable. When that sheep is found (discovers its spiritual
nature), great joy is experienced by the sheep and the shepherd.

We also find the use of allegory throughout the Old
Testament. These verses from the book of Isaiah are known as
the Parable of the Vineyard:

> "Let me sing for my beloved
>   my love-song concerning his
>   vineyard:
> My beloved had a vineyard
>   on a very fertile hill.
> He dug it and cleared it of stones,
>   and planted it with choice vines;
> he built a watchtower in the midst
>   of it,
>   and hewed out a wine vat in it;
> he expected it to yield grapes,
>   but it yielded wild grapes.
>
> And now, inhabitants of Jerusalem
>   and people of Judah,
> judge between me
>   and my vineyard.

What more was there to do for my
vineyard
that I have not done in it?
When I expected it to yield grapes,
why did it yield wild grapes?

And now I will tell you
what I will do to my vineyard.
I will remove its hedge,
and it shall be devoured;
I will break down its wall,
and it shall be trampled down.
I will make it a waste;
it shall not be pruned or hoed,
and it shall be overgrown with
briers and thorns;
I will also command the clouds
that they rain no rain upon it.

For the vineyard of the Lord of hosts
is the house of Israel,
and the people of Judah
are his pleasant planting;
he expected justice,
but saw bloodshed;
righteousness,
but heard a cry!"[22]

This passage is not only allegorical but explains its meaning in the final sentence. Isaiah was attempting to describe the initial and current moral character of the nation of Israel through the symbology of the vineyard. Originally, Israel had a bright future, like a vineyard that was fertile, meticulously prepared, planted with the best vines, given good security (watchtower), and a winepress. The vineyard had all the makings of a fine wine-producing business. Unfortunately, even after all the painstaking preparation, the vineyard produced wild or sour grapes. Isaiah throws this case before the very people presented in the parable and then proceeds to tell them of their own destruction. Interestingly, from a Hebrew language perspective, the words for justice, bloodshed, and righteousness all sound very much alike. This play on words provided the icing on the cake of Isaiah's prophecy. Personally interpreted, this parable applies to someone who, through free choice, has wasted his or her potential for good.

Through the use of the allegorical interpretive lens, we are searching for basic life truths beyond the concrete elements of the story. As with other lenses, not all Bible verses can be interpreted allegorically. Look for passages that contain imagery, parables, poetry, song, or ones that are not easily understood in a plain, logical sense.[23]

Prophetic

Prophetic vision has always been a part of the human experience. Through an inner sight, people have seen images of potential futures. In some cases, these prophecies have been literal, directly corresponding to future events. Through an intuitive vision, a seer might see the image of an airplane crashing in a certain part of the world, foretelling the actual event. However, prophecy often involves the interpretation of imagery that is highly symbolic in nature. For a moment, just suppose you are at a movie theater watching these images portrayed on the screen:

A bloodthirsty, seven-headed, red dragon leaps across the field chasing after the mother of a newborn, male child. The screams of frightened teenaged girls fill the room as they clutch their boyfriends' arms for dear life. The scene suddenly shifts as a horde of warriors, mounted on lion headed steeds, two hundred million strong, fan out across the earth killing one in three people in their path. Those who escape the fire, smoke, and brimstone[24] spewing from the horses' mouths meet their doom by the bite of their snakelike tails.

The cinematic carnage continues as evil, wicked, despotic rulers with massive armies war against each other, resulting in widespread famine and disease. Then, Mother Nature unleashes her fury by triggering earthquakes so cataclysmic that they level entire mountains. Weather becomes erratic and turbulent as torrents of rain, hailstones up to one hundred pounds in weight, fire, and good old brimstone come crashing to the ground, devastating practically everything left standing on the surface of the earth. Finally, the movie ends as scorpion-tailed locusts swoop down from the sky, stinging whoever is still left alive. THE END. (Thank God!)

If this wasn't a Bible study handbook, you would probably think that these are scenes from some grade-C sci-fi horror flick. But you guessed it, it is just our friend, the Bible. In fact, all the images presented were comprised from these Bible verses:

Seven-headed red dragon—Revelation 12:3–17

Two hundred million warriors on lion-headed horses—Revelation 9:15–19

Rulers with massive armies—Daniel 11

War, famines, plagues, earthquakes—Matthew 24:7, Mark 13:8, Luke 21:11

Cataclysmic earthquakes, rain, hailstones, fire, sulphur—Ezekiel 38:20, 22

One hundred pound hailstones—Revelation 16:21

Scorpion-like locusts—Revelation 9:3–11

The Bible contains numerous prophetic writings. Fifteen Old Testament books are personally attributed to prophets. The accomplishments of the prophets Elijah and Elisha are found in the books of 1 and 2 Kings. Other prophetic writings are found throughout the Bible, especially in the books of Daniel, Revelation, and all The Gospels.

Many biblical prophecies are apocalyptic, as shown in the

aforementioned examples. These prophecies forecast end times, hellacious battles, Judgment Day, and other melancholy possibilities. However, not all Bible prophecy is doom and gloom. Intuitive vision also unveils a more encouraging outlook. Moses received a divine message about "a land flowing with milk and honey."[25] Jesus foresaw a time when human beings would accomplish incredible feats: "Very truly, I tell you, the one who believes in me will also do the works that I do and, in fact, will do greater works than these."[26]

When we view the Bible through the prophetic interpretive lens, we always must be mindful of the primary audience of its oracles. In the majority of cases, these prophecies foretold events of ancient times. For example, Jeremiah's prophecies warned the people of Judah about the impending invasion by the Babylonians. Unfortunately, these warnings went entirely unheeded, as indicated by Jeremiah's description of his immediate listeners: "Hear this, O foolish and senseless people, who have eyes, but do not see, who have ears, but do not hear."[27] Remember, we are not the foolish and senseless people of Jeremiah's admonishment.

However, we may feel as if we are. We may wonder, why does Jeremiah appear to be speaking to us? Do his words, spoken some 2600 years ago, apply to our future too? It is not uncommon for us modern people to personally relate to ancient prophecies. Many prophecies taken out of context seem strangely applicable to our current era. There are some possible explanations for this transference of relevance:

(1) Because of the cyclical nature of history, prophecies have a universal quality. Events of the past are destined to reoccur many times in the future. Names may change, technology may advance, but the human experience repeats itself. Therefore an ancient prophecy may be applied to multiple time periods. Anyone living in a country with an aggressive northerly neighbor might feel an inner pang of anxiety upon reading this prophecy:

"The word of the Lord came to me a second time, saying, 'What do you see?' And I said, 'I see a boiling pot, tilted away from the north.' Then the Lord said to me: Out of the north disaster shall break out on all the inhabitants of the land."[28]

Survivors of a major earthquake might find themselves relating to this prophecy of Jeremiah:

"I looked on the earth, and lo, it was
         waste and void;
      and to the heavens, and they had
         no light.
   I looked on the mountains, and lo,
         they were quaking,
      and all the hills moved to and fro.
   I looked, and lo, there was no one at all,
      and all the birds of the air had fled.
   I looked, and lo, the fruitful land
         was a desert,
      and all its cities were laid in ruins
      before the Lord, before his fierce anger."[29]

(2) Perhaps ancient prophecies do speak directly about future events in modern times. It is certainly conceivable that the intuitive vision of an ancient seer could extend beyond his or her immediate future. These prophecies may even include more than one outcome of the same prophecy. Let us consider another of Jeremiah's predictions:

"Return, O faithless children, says the Lord,
         for I am your master;
      I will take you, one from a city and two from a
         family,
      and I will bring you to Zion.

"I will give you shepherds after my own heart, who will feed you with knowledge and understanding. And when you have multiplied and increased in the land, in those days, says the Lord, they shall no longer say, 'The ark of the covenant of the Lord.' It shall not come to mind, or be remembered, or missed; nor shall another one be made. At that time Jerusalem shall be called the throne of the Lord, and all nations shall gather to it, to the presence of the Lord in Jerusalem, and they shall no longer stubbornly follow their own evil will. In those days the house of Judah shall join the house of Israel, and together they shall come from the land of the north to the land that I gave your ancestors for a heritage."[30]

This prophecy could be applied to two different periods of time. Initially, it probably spoke to the return of the exiles from Babylon and the eventual reunification of the Northern and Southern kingdoms. However, might it also allude to the twentieth-century establishment of the modern state of Israel?

(3) Although biblical prophecies usually relate directly to an immediate audience, their symbolism can be indirectly linked to the experiences of future generations. For an example of this kind of prophetic symbolism, let us turn to an Apocryphal book, 2 Esdras:

"On the second night I had a vision in a dream; I saw, rising from the sea, an eagle with twelve wings and three heads. I saw it spread its wings over the whole earth; and all the winds blew on it, and the clouds gathered. Out of its wings I saw rival wings sprout, which proved to be only small and stunted. Its heads lay still; even the middle head, which was bigger than the others, lay still between them. As I watched, the eagle rose on its wings to set itself up as ruler over the earth and its inhabitants. I saw it bring into subjection everything under heaven; it met with no opposition at all from any creature on earth."[31]

This writing is characteristic of the symbology found in Bible prophecy. The eagle is not a literal figure (unless you've seen a three-headed eagle flying around lately) but represents something far more realistic. A further reading of the narrative reveals details that help interpret the images. Interestingly, the twelfth chapter of 2 Esdras specifically interprets this terrifying, apocalyptic vision for its readers. The eagle represents the expansion and dominance of the Roman Empire. Its three heads and twelve wings depict various ruling factions and reigning periods within the history of the Empire.

The vision culminates with the entrance of a lion who says to the eagle:

> "You have oppressed the gentle and injured the peaceful, hating the truthful and loving liars; you have destroyed the homes of the prosperous, and razed to the ground the walls of those who had done you no harm. . . . So you, eagle, must now disappear and be seen no more, you and your terrible great wings, your evil small wings, your cruel heads, your grim talons, and your whole worthless body. Then all the earth will feel relief at its deliverance from your violence, and look forward hopefully to the judgment and mercy of its Creator."[32]

A modern reader of this prophecy might find its symbology eerily consistent with the rise and fall of a twentieth-century menace. While the eagle was the military symbol of the Roman Empire, it was also a prominent emblem of Nazi Germany. The lion of the book of Esdras refers to a supernatural, Messianic figure. A contemporary interpretation would suggest that the lion was the allied force that defeated Hitler in World War II. In both scenarios, the Roman and Nazi empires were destroyed, thus fulfilling the prophecy.

As we consider these explanations for our fascination and acceptance of ancient prophecies, you may notice an interconnectedness between them. They each attempt to logically demonstrate how our attempts to decode the prophetic cipher may be relevant. What are we looking for? We are looking to the past to explain our own future. We hope and pray that these writings hold the key to knowing what is in store for us as a civilization. This is the nature of modern biblical prophecy. Our task as Bible students is to intelligently discern whether the prophecies are distinctly ancient, universally applicable, or point to our era. Once we determine the answer, we can use our own intuitive deciphering faculty to unlock the messages of the ancient writings and convert them into usable present-day information.

Metaphysical

For many metaphysical Christians, the primary purpose of life is to know ourselves fully. We ask the proverbial question: Who am I? The answer lies beneath the surface level of human existence. When we reach that point in our spiritual quest where we recognize that our identity must be more than our physical bodies, emotional ups and downs, and intellectual faculties, we enter the metaphysical world.

For most people, the word *metaphysical* is a spooky one. We fear it and yet are intrigued by it. Simply understood, metaphysical describes the realm of existence beyond what we can perceive through our external senses. A more palatable term for metaphysical is *spiritual*.

The metaphysical interpretive lens is the most important of all. For that reason, Chapter 9 is entirely devoted to it. All the tools of Bible study, all the interpretive lenses are at our disposal for a singular purpose—to interpret the Bible metaphysically. Why? Because, metaphysical Bible interpretation allows us to embrace scripture at our spiritual core, at that place where we ask the question: Who am I? In the process, we discover that the Bible is a story about our spiritual destiny.

Metaphysical Bible interpretation is an inward journey into the soul of humanity. Through it, we grasp the psychology of our spiritual journey. We begin by asking: How do the characters, objects, places, and activities in the Bible relate to our spiritual growth?

For example:

> "And he told them many things in parables, saying: 'Listen! A sower went out to sow. And as he sowed, some seeds fell on the path, and the birds came and ate them up. Other seeds fell on rocky ground, where they did not have much soil, and they sprang up quickly, since they had no depth of soil. But when the sun rose, they were scorched; and since they had no root, they withered away. Other seeds fell among thorns, and the thorns grew up and choked them. Other seeds fell on good soil and brought forth grain, some a hundredfold, some sixty, some thirty. Let anyone with ears listen!'"[33]

From a factual, physical perspective, this story illustrates the viability of different soils for growing plants. Allegorically speaking, we have discovered that parables usually have a deeper, less obvious meaning. In this case, the soils represent various people and their ability to accept Jesus Christ and his message (seeds). Only the people whose soil is good are able to utilize his message in living their lives. The other people are either too flighty or superficial (on path eaten by birds), too set in their ways (hard), or too contentious (thorny) to listen to the gospel.

Metaphysical interpretation takes us another step deeper than the allegorical. It brings us into a process of identifying those components of the story that represent mental states of consciousness, spiritual awareness, and universal laws. Applied to the Parable of the Sower, the metaphysical interpretive lens reveals to us a story about our receptivity (soil) to spiritual ideas (seed). If we are to advance spiritually, we must become like the good soil, willing to listen to the inner prompting of God's spirit. Spiritual ideas will not take hold unless there is this fertility of consciousness. We must prepare the soil of our minds as a farmer would ready a field for planting. It must be cultivated with the utmost care. Likewise, we are compelled to be vigilant by being inwardly conscious of God's ideas and ready to allow them to become a part of our experience. If we are lazy in our spiritual practice, the soil of our minds may deteriorate to the point where the ideas will not become well rooted and, therefore, not grow to full maturity. This was the fate of the seed that fell on the other soils. Our spiritual growth becomes fulfilled as we become careful gardeners of our inner, mental fields and cooperate with the law of mind action.

The law of mind action is probably the most important principle of metaphysical Christianity. Unity minister Hypatia Hasbrouck explains the law:

> *Thoughts held in mind produce after their kind.* This statement means that if we persistently think a particular kind of thought, other thoughts of the same kind will form in our minds, and eventually we will feel compelled to say the words or do the acts that express the thoughts outwardly so that corresponding conditions or things will be formed in us or in our

environment. It also means that we may attract to ourselves or be drawn toward conditions, persons, and things that reflect our persistent thoughts.[34]

A Story as Seen Through the Nine Interpretive Lenses

The parable of the Prodigal Son:

"Then Jesus said, 'There was a man who had two sons. The younger of them said to his father, "Father, give me the share of the property that will belong to me." So he divided his property between them. A few days later the younger son gathered all he had and traveled to a distant country, and there he squandered his property in dissolute living. When he had spent everything, a severe famine took place throughout that country, and he began to be in need. So he went and hired himself out to one of the citizens of that country, who sent him to his fields to feed the pigs. He would gladly have filled himself with the pods that the pigs were eating; and no one gave him anything. But when he came to himself he said, "How many of my father's hired hands have bread enough and to spare, but here I am dying of hunger! I will get up and go to my father, and I will say to him, 'Father, I have sinned against heaven and before you; I am no longer worthy to be called your son; treat me like one of your hired hands.'" So he set off and went to his father. But while he was still far off, his father saw him and was filled with compassion; he ran and put his arms around him and kissed him. Then the son said to him, "Father, I have sinned against heaven and before you; I am no longer worthy to be called your son." But the father said to his slaves, "Quickly,

bring out a robe—the best one—and put it on him;
put a ring on his finger and sandals on his feet. And
get the fatted calf and kill it, and let us eat and celebrate; for this son of mine was dead and is alive
again; he was lost and is found!" And they began to
celebrate. Now his elder son was in the field; and
when he came and approached the house, he heard
music and dancing. He called one of the slaves and
asked what was going on. He replied, "Your brother
has come, and your father has killed the fatted calf,
because he has got him back safe and sound." Then
he became angry and refused to go in. His father
came out and began to plead with him. But he answered his father, "Listen! For all these years I have
been working like a slave for you, and I have never
disobeyed your command; yet you have never given
me even a young goat so that I might celebrate with
my friends. But when this son of yours came back,
who has devoured your property with prostitutes,
you killed the fatted calf for him!" Then the father
said to him, "Son, you are always with me, and all
that is mine is yours. But we had to celebrate and rejoice, because this brother of yours was dead and has
come to life; he was lost and has been found."'"[35]

Here are some possible interpretations:

Factual: The story could be true. It happened just the way
we read it. This kind of thing has happened in families before.

Historical: Jesus retells the story with some embellishment
(i.e., best robe, fatted calf, big party) to make it more interesting and convincing.

Dramatic: All three characters have an internal drama going
on. Young son: Overcomes shame in returning home. Older
son: Faces his angry, jealous, goody-two-shoes attitude toward
his brother and father. Father: Presented his sons with an op-

portunity to be forgiving and understanding of each other. He experiences grief at his son's leaving and joy at his return.

Comedic: This story has a humorous moment when the young son is forced to slop hogs for a living. Can you imagine him falling down in the mud with pigs snorting in his face?

Literary: This story reads very easily and contains rich images and messages for its readers.

Moral: The youngest son discovered that his father was more generous and forgiving than he thought. The older son learned that outer goodness must be complimented by an inner peace, love, and self-acceptance. The moral of the story: People are better than we assume them to be.

Allegorical: This story is not about one family but about the ideal community. The father is the community leadership, providing sufficiently for the needs of its people (the sons) regardless of their past mistakes and decisions.

Prophetic: This story tells of a day when all parents will love their children as unconditionally as the father in the story.

Metaphysical: The story is a lesson in prosperity. Father = God's everlasting, all-providing love and substance; Young son = openness in attracting good but is poor at managing prosperity; Older son = self-enslaved, self-absorbed consciousness, unwilling to venture beyond the comfort zones, too internally focused; Robe, fatted calf, and the ring = the basic necessities of life (clothing, food, and money).

Summary

By now you should realize that Bible reading always involves interpretation and that any attempt to read the Bible *literally* will result in failure. The Bible's richness and complexity touch us on many levels. Hopefully this chapter has described for you a number of interpretive options at your disposal in discerning these levels. The lens you select depends on your needs and inclinations. Always be aware that your comprehension of the Bible is directly determined by the nature of your interpretive lens. You broaden your understanding of a passage or story by looking through more than one interpretive lens. Quite simply, if you want to see something new, change lenses.

This chapter has only touched upon the most significant interpretive lens, the metaphysical, or spiritual. Read on to Chapter 9 for a more in-depth look at metaphysical Bible interpretation.

Notes

1. Although the last Studebaker car rolled off the assembly line in 1966, I have used it in this example in an effort not to promote the purchase of any car currently in production. Resemblance to the author's name is purely intentional!

2. The writings of the first-century C.E. Jewish historian Josephus provide the Bible student with some third-party credibility regarding biblical facts.

3. John 11:35, KJV.

4. Exodus 37:1.

5. 1 Chronicles 20:5.

6. Genesis 29:16–25.

7. Genesis 38:12–26.

8. Judges 16:4–19.

9. 2 Samuel 11:2–27.

10. John 8:3–11.

11. Matthew 26:3–57.

12. Acts 16:26–39.

13. 1 Samuel 15:19, and thirty other verses from the books of Samuel and Kings.

14. Director of the famous 1950s movie *The Ten Commandments,* starring Charlton Heston as Moses.

15. This is actually two stories spliced together into one. Other versions can be found in Matthew 17:14–21 and Luke 9:37–43.

16. Comedian Bill Cosby performed a very funny rendition of Noah's Ark.

17. Refer to *The Virtues Guide—A Handbook for Parents Teaching Virtues,* by Linda Kavelin Popov, Dan Popov, and John Kavelin. The book is published by Personal Power Press International, Inc., Box V-49 RR#1, Bowen Island, B.C. V0N 1G0, Canada.

18. Luke 6:31. See also Matthew 7:12.

19. This phrase is a common English idiomatic expression.

20. Causative. Explains how things came to be the way they are today.

21. Luke 15:3–7.

22. Isaiah 5:1–7.

23. See Galatians 4:21–31 for an allegorical interpretation of an Old Testament story.

24. What is brimstone, anyway? Answer: sulfur. In the Bible, brimstone is usually accompanied by fire. Sulfur is highly flammable and creates a noxious gas when burned. Volcanic eruptions usually contain sulfurous gas.

25. Exodus 3:8 and elsewhere.

26. John 14:12.

27. Jeremiah 5:21.

28. Jeremiah 1:13–14.

29. Jeremiah 4:23–26.

30. Jeremiah 3:14–18.

31. 2 Esdras 11:1–6, NEB.

32. 2 Esdras 11:42–46, NEB.

33. Matthew 13:3–9.

34. Hypatia Hasbrouck, *Handbook of Positive Prayer* (Unity Village, Mo.: Unity Books, 1995), p. 9.

35. Luke 15:11–32.

Chapter 9

The Uniqueness of Metaphysical Interpretation

W isdom for a Lifetime also could have been subtitled *A Metaphysical Christian's Guide to Bible Study.* You likely consider yourself to be metaphysically oriented, have read some books on the subject, or have attended a class, program, or workshop presented by a metaphysical speaker. If you are like most metaphysical people, you have an almost insatiable appetite for spiritual knowledge. However, in all likelihood, the spiritual insights you have attained may not have had much in the way of a biblical element. *Wisdom for a Lifetime* seeks to change that deficiency.

Since this book also purports to teach you *how* to fish, your reading progress indicates that you are ready to do some deep-sea fishing, that is, interpret the Bible for your own spiritual growth. The steps outlined in this chapter will enable you to uncover for yourself the spiritual treasure hidden in the Bible.

Defining Metaphysical

The word *metaphysical* is one that evokes a variety of responses. Some people view this word with suspicion or puzzlement. It could be that they have heard hard-line ministers preach tirades against dabbling in metaphysical studies, usually calling it the work of the devil. To others, *metaphysical* is a word shrouded in mystery and not a part of one's everyday vocabulary. However, there is an increasing acceptance of metaphysical subjects among the general public. Major booksellers regularly stock popular metaphysical books. Computer on-line services have established folders and forums for metaphysical discussion. Nationally broadcast television shows have interviewed metaphysical authors.[1] Metaphysics is no longer a *verboten* subject in our society. So, what makes the metaphysical perspective unique?

Consider the many utility services connected to your household. If, for instance, you neglect to pay your cable TV bill, your service will likely be turned off. Gone are your favorite channels and programs. Reconnection requires the payment of the fees due. When the financial requirements are met, the service is restored, and once again you can enjoy the benefits of cable television.

> **"Christ in you, the hope of glory."**
> —Colossians 1:27

There is a similarity between utility service and our relationship with God. In the beginning, our souls began their sojourn as offspring of the divine Creator.[2] However, difficult life circumstances, an erroneous belief in a primordial unworthiness, and other misconceptions led many to feel isolated from the Supreme Being. We became temporarily disconnected from God, forgetful of our spiritual heritage. Something had to be done to redeem humanity from its fallen state, to re-establish a link between God and His most prized creation. Religion became the answer. By following the dictates of the prevailing religion, one could be reasonably assured of spiritual reconnection. From Genesis to Revelation, the theme of redemption pervades the entire Bible.

The methods of re-establishing connection with God diverge greatly among religious groups. Generally speaking, Jews observe numerous dietary and cultural laws and celebrate special holidays. Many Catholic Christians follow prescribed rituals and repeat certain prayers. Most Protestant Christians espouse strict Bible study and faith in Jesus Christ. As you can see, the utility reconnection fees vary, depending upon one's individual religious beliefs and practices.

Metaphysically speaking, redemption is not so much a matter of pleasing God through specific actions but of simply changing one's mind or consciousness. When individual awareness transcends the physical, material world to embrace spiritual reality at the core of one's Self, redemption occurs. Where traditional religion sees God and humanity as separate items—one perfect, the other flawed—the metaphysically minded person views the two as inseparable and intertwined. Through the redemption of consciousness, one no longer perceives a division between God and humanity but instead sees oneself as a direct and perfect expression of God. The spiritual character of humanity remains constant, only individual awareness and perception change.

> **"Rejoice always, pray without ceasing, give thanks in all circumstances."**
> —1 Thessalonians 5:16–18

Recall this scene from the gospel of John when Jesus said:

> "'The Father and I are one.' The Jews took up stones again to stone him. Jesus replied, 'I have shown you many good works from the Father. For which of these are you going to stone me?' The Jews answered, 'It is not for a good work that we are going to stone you, but for blasphemy, because you, though only a human being, are making yourself God.' Jesus answered, 'Is it not written in your law, "I said, you are gods"? [Psalm 82:6] If those to whom the word of God came were called "gods"—and the scripture cannot be annulled—can you say that the one whom the Father has sanctified and sent into

the world is blaspheming because I said, "I am God's Son"? If I am not doing the works of my Father, then do not believe me. But if I do them, even though you do not believe me, believe the works, so that you may know and understand that the Father is in me and I am in the Father.' Then they tried to arrest him again, but he escaped from their hands."[3]

This passage demonstrates the metaphysical perspective regarding the spiritual nature of humanity. Jesus represents the perfected human being who knows his spiritual identity. His works and miracles are testimony to his conscious relationship with God. The Jews represent the traditional view of human and divine separateness, a view that they hold to with great tenacity even to the point of trying to kill Jesus. However, Jesus prevails, and the Jews walk away empty-handed except for their mistaken beliefs.

> **"For everything created by God is good."**
> —1 Timothy 4:4

Jesus is the model, the Way-Shower, the Master Teacher. Redemption from a sense of separateness comes by following his example, his way, his teachings. Eventually, we reach the point in consciousness where we recognize the same truth Jesus did: "the Father and I are one."

For the metaphysical Christian, one's life purpose becomes an adventure, a journey that leads to the revelation that humanity has always been one with God. Given this mind-set, the *utility hookup* for metaphysical Christians involves a commitment to those spiritual practices that help to reaffirm one's oneness with God—namely, regular prayer, meditation, study, and personal reflection. Redemption is an ongoing process leading to a more permanent awareness of God's presence. This experience is key to the metaphysically minded person.

Another primary aspect of metaphysics is the function of the mind in creation. This understanding is based on the law of mind action that was defined in chapter eight.[4] Poetically put:

Thoughts held in mind produce after their kind. In other words, what we think about all day, either positively or negatively, usually happens to us. Unless, of course, we change the character of our thoughts and create a whole different experience for ourselves.

Biblically, there is much support for this law. Each of these passages describes how this law applies to us:

> "You will decide on a matter, and it will be established for you, and light will shine on your ways."[5] "For as he thinketh in his heart, so is he:"[6] "Ask, and it will be given you; search, and you will find; knock, and the door will be opened for you. For everyone who asks receives, and everyone who searches finds, and for everyone who knocks, the door will be opened."[7]

The thoughts we give the most power to are *established* for us in the arena of life. Thoughts of love, acceptance, and peace produce constructive and fulfilling experiences. Moreover, according to the same principle, fear, worry, and pessimism draw to us challenging circumstances. The degree of emotional energy we invest in our thoughts determines the intensity and durability of our experience. Recall the words of Job:

> "Truly the thing that I fear comes upon me,
> and what I dread befalls me.
> I am not at ease, nor am I quiet;
> I have no rest; but trouble comes."[8]

These two factors, the innate divinity and goodness of humanity and the law of mind action, are fundamental to the metaphysical outlook. Keep these ideas at the forefront of your mind as you study the Bible through the metaphysical interpretive lens.

Metaphysical Bible Interpretation

The metaphysical interpretation of the Bible has been around for a long time. It is nothing new. For millennia, mystics and metaphysically minded people have looked into the scriptures and have seen a spiritual dimension and meaning beyond conventional understanding. Their discoveries nourished their souls and encouraged them in their pursuit of God awareness. For example, the author of *The Cloud of Unknowing*[9] metaphysically interpreted the story of Martha and Mary from Luke 10:38–42 to explain the nature of the contemplative life. He wrote:

> In the Gospel of St. Luke we read that our Lord came to Martha's house and while she set about at once to prepare his meal, her sister Mary did nothing but sit at his feet. She was so intent upon listening to him that she paid no attention to what Martha was doing. Now certainly Martha's chores were holy and important. (Indeed, they are the works of the first degree of the active life.) But Mary was unconcerned about them. Neither did she notice our Lord's human bearing, the beauty of his mortal body, or the sweetness of his human voice and conversation. . . . But she forgot all of this and was totally absorbed in the highest wisdom of God concealed in the obscurity of his humanity. . . .
>
> My friend, do you see that this whole incident concerning Jesus and the two sisters was intended as a lesson for active and contemplative persons of the Church in every age? Mary represents the contemplative life and all contemplative persons ought to model their lives on hers. Martha represents the active life and all active persons should take her as their guide.[10]

Our purpose in interpreting the Bible metaphysically is to delve beneath the obvious to the not-so-obvious meaning of the scriptures. As we grow spiritually, our enhanced awareness allows us to grasp the metaphysical significance of our lives. When applied to biblical study, we suddenly perceive and understand the deeper, spiritual intent behind the words on the page. It is as if by magic that these words come alive as they never did before. The people, stories, and passages spring forth—reminding us of our own spiritual journey, our own life process. A spiritual connection and correspondence unfolds from within us. A biblical character's trials and overcomings instantly become our own inner struggles and breakthroughs. The Bible immediately hits home at a personal soul level, that is, it becomes relevant. No longer does it gather dust on the shelf but becomes an invaluable resource, a handbook for living, for it enhances and reaffirms our understanding of spiritual Truth.

For example, return to the Martha and Mary story mentioned earlier. After reading this story, you may feel yourself closely identifying with one of these characters. Let's say that you have been pretty busy at work. You have had to attend to numerous details, and you are high on stress and low on energy. More than likely you will favor Martha. You may envy those people who seem to have time for spiritual study, class attendance, and meditation. If, on the other hand, your life is in balance, you enter into each day relaxed, and you spend plenty of time in prayer, you will find that Mary will speak to you the most. Depending on the circumstances of our lives, these characters reach us at our deepest soul level. This is another important aspect of metaphysical interpretation.

The metaphysical interpretive lens nearly always employs an allegorical, psychological, and spiritual aspect in its use. Ask yourself certain questions: How does the biblical story relate to human thinking? What's going on in the consciousness of a person? What universal laws are operative? What do the characters symbolize in my mind? How does this story relate to my spiritual growth? The process is very similar to dream in-terpretation. Metaphysically, the people, places, things, and actions each repre-sent thoughts in the mind rather than lit-eral objects and occurrences.

"For God did not give us a spirit of cowardice, but rather a spirit of power and of love and of self-discipline."
—2 Timothy 1:7

Sometimes the interpretation actually relates to the content of the story, but in many cases the meaning is taken out of context. Even if metaphysical interpretation was not the aim of the biblical writers, a metaphysical message often manages to come through regardless of original intent. The non-relatedness of a Bible story with a metaphysical interpretation is always di-rected by the mental orientation of the Bible interpreter. This is true of all Bible interpretation.

For instance, let us examine this familiar verse from the book of Isaiah: "For unto us a child is born, unto us a son is given: and the government shall be upon his shoulder: and his name shall be called Wonderful, Counsellor, The mighty God, The everlasting Father, The Prince of Peace."[11]

How often have you heard this passage read at a Christmas season service? Most Christians accept this prophecy to mean the coming of Jesus Christ hundreds of years in the future.[12] Metaphysically, we might interpret this passage as alluding to the emerging awareness of God's Spirit within—a Presence that counsels, guides, and protects wherever we are. How-ever, most scholars agree that the original intent of the verse was to announce Isaiah's prophecy of a new Davidic ruler who would restore the Jewish nation back into God's good graces.

This kind of out-of-context interpretation, metaphysical or not, is common to all Bible interpretation. Spiritual insights al-ways emerge through our own perception, the lenses of our own consciousness. We see what our minds want to see. You just never know what you will see in a Bible passage. Remember the red Studebakers from Chapter 8?

The early New Thought writers may not have invented metaphysical Bible interpretation, but they certainly refined it. Through their efforts, metaphysical interpretation has been proven to be a valid, effective, and legitimate method of scriptural study. Review Chapter 4, "Metaphysical Christianity's Biblical Heritage," for a detailed examination of their writings. Consider including any or all of their books in your Bible study library.

Assembling a Metaphysical Bible Study Tool Kit

It is now time for all the chapters of this book to come together in unison. Their sole purpose is to help you, the Bible student, perform your own biblical interpretations. The following is a suggested metaphysical Bible study tool kit with corresponding chapter references:

Chapter 4—Metaphysical Christianity's Biblical Heritage

Metaphysical Bible Dictionary
Let There Be Light
Your Hope of Glory
Be Ye Transformed
The Sermon on the Mount

Chapter 5—Getting Started

A good study Bible of one of the recommended translations (Computer users add a Bible program)

Chapter 6—Making a Bible Study Tool Kit

Bible Concordance (corresponding with your Bible
    translation)[13]
Bible Dictionary (single or multiple volume)
Bible Commentary (single or multiple volume)
Bible Atlas
Bible Handbook

Chapter 7—Close to the Source

Strong's Exhaustive Concordance of the Bible

Chapter 8—Everyone Interprets the Bible

Review the nine interpretive lenses:
(1) Factual
(2) Historical
(3) Dramatic
(4) Comedic
(5) Literary
(6) Moral
(7) Allegorical
(8) Prophetic
(9) Metaphysical

With all these resources at your disposal, you will be able to
metaphysically interpret any Bible story or verse and effectively
apply that interpretation directly to your personal life. Your only
other preparation is to be consciously attuned to your own
inner, spiritual journey and process.

Four-Step Process of Metaphysical Bible Interpretation

Equipped with the Metaphysical Bible Study Tool Kit, here is a four-step procedure that will help you organize your interpretations of the Bible:

STEP ONE: SELECT, READ, AND STUDY THE SCRIPTURE

- Select the passage(s) to be studied
- Read the passage(s) several times
- Consult a Bible dictionary for general information on distinctive or unfamiliar words
- Consult Bible commentaries and handbooks for historical and scholastic information on the biblical book, chapter, and verse
- Consult a Bible atlas to determine the location of the biblical event
- Gain a basic understanding of the story line

STEP TWO: IDENTIFY THE KEY WORDS AND PHRASES

- Scan the passage for those verses and words that you feel are most important to the meaning of the story line or are unique in character:
- Nouns: proper names, people, places, objects, animals
- Verbs: actions, movement, thought, feeling
- Other words or phrases that are descriptive of the scene

STEP THREE: DEVELOP INTERPRETATIONS FOR THE WORDS

- Consult the *Metaphysical Bible Dictionary* for suggested interpretations of proper names, name places, and special words (i.e., Adam, Jesus, Egypt, Nazareth, Logos, serpent, etc.)
- Consult an English dictionary (such as *Webster's Dictionary*) and a thesaurus for the meaning of and synonyms for common words (i.e., assurance, good, judgment, lyre, righteousness, treasure, etc.)

- Use *Strong's Concordance*'s Hebrew and Greek dictionaries to obtain exegetical information on selected words
- Consider how the words represent states of consciousness (i.e., doubt, faith, love, praise, temptation, etc.)

STEP FOUR: ALLOW THE METAPHYSICAL MEANING TO EMERGE

- Study, pray, and meditate on the overall story and the individual words interpreted in STEP THREE
- Consult metaphysical interpretation books that interpret the selected passage(s)
- Think about how these states of consciousness might correspond to events in your own life (i.e., healing of illness, conquering financial problems, dealing with persecution, feeling an overwhelming sense of joy, etc.)
- Utilize the many interpretive lenses (i.e., factual, historical, dramatic, comedic, etc.)
- Explore common metaphysical themes (i.e., illumination, healing, prosperity, etc.) as they might apply
- Apply your own innate creative intelligence—look at the story from many vantage points and perspectives
- Remember, the metaphysical interpretive lens has an allegorical, psychological, and spiritual dimension
- Finally, ask yourself, what jumps out at you about the passage? What clicks in you when you read it? Look for the personal, spiritual dimension that rises to the surface of your mind
- Write down your interpretation as soon as it is revealed to you

How to Use the Four-Step Process

The following is a systematic, thorough, metaphysical interpretation of a familiar New Testament Bible story using the Four-Step Process. Each of the steps and suggested approaches have been included for easy reference and practical repetition.

STEP ONE: SELECT, READ, AND STUDY THE SCRIPTURE

• **Select the passage(s) to be studied:** Mark 10:13–16, Jesus blesses the children. The New Revised Standard Version will be the translation used to select words for interpretation.
• **Read the passage(s) several times:**

> "People were bringing little children to him in order that he might touch them; and the disciples spoke sternly to them. But when Jesus saw this, he was indignant and said to them, 'Let the little children come to me; do not stop them; for it is to such as these that the kingdom of God belongs. Truly I tell you, whoever does not receive the kingdom of God as a little child will never enter it.' And he took them up in his arms, laid his hands on them, and blessed them."

• **Consult a Bible dictionary for general information on distinctive or unfamiliar words:** Look up *Jesus (Jesus Christ), disciples, kingdom of God.*
• **Consult Bible commentaries and handbooks for historical and scholastic information on the biblical book, chapter, and verses:** This same story can also be found in Matthew 19:13–15 and Luke 18:15–17. However, the story from Mark adds one additional feature not found in the others: Jesus' indignation toward his disciples.
• **Consult a Bible atlas to determine the location of the biblical event:** Clues regarding the location of this story are found in two previous verses. Mark 9:33 reads, "Then they came to Capernaum." Mark 10:1 reads, "He left that place and went to the region of Judea and beyond the Jordan."

Given this information, Jesus must have left Capernaum, on the northern shore of the Sea of Galilee, and headed south. He either traveled through Samaria and crossed the

Jordan River from Judea, or he circled around the Sea of Galilee and headed down the east bank of the river. Some scholars suggest that he may have avoided Samaria as many Jews did and opted for the latter route. Since Jesus' final destination was Jerusalem (see Mark 10:32), and he apparently entered the city from the east through Bethany and Bethphage (see Mark 11:1), it is probable that he arrived there from the east. The region to the east of Judea across the Jordan River was called Perea (present-day Jordan) and was the likely location for this story.

• **Gain a basic understanding of the story line:** This story has two distinct qualities. First, the story depicts a loving, tender moment between Jesus and the children. In ancient cultures, children (and women) were not held in as high esteem as they are today. Jesus' interest in their welfare marks a change in attitude. Secondly, Jesus turns this gathering into a classroom to reveal the qualifications of those who experience the kingdom of God. The disciples are the prime focus of his teaching.

STEP TWO: IDENTIFY THE KEY WORDS AND PHRASES

• **Scan the passage for those verses and words that you feel are most important to the meaning of the story line or are unique in character, listed in the order they appear in the text.**

• **Nouns: proper names, people, places, objects, animals:** *people, little children, disciples, Jesus, kingdom of God*

• **Verbs: actions, movements, thoughts, feelings:** *bringing, touch, spoke sternly, indignant, stop, tell, receive, enter, took, blessed*

• **Other words or phrases that are descriptive of the scene:** *truly, never*

STEP THREE: DEVELOP INTERPRETATIONS FOR THE WORDS

- **Consult the *Metaphysical Bible Dictionary* for suggested interpretations of proper names, name places, and special words (i.e., *people, disciples, Jesus, Kingdom*)**
- **Consult an English dictionary (such as *Webster's Dictionary*) and a thesaurus for the meaning of and synonyms for common words (i.e., *little children, stop, never*)**
- **Use *Strong's Concordance*'s Hebrew and Greek dictionaries to obtain exegetical information on selected words**
- **Consider how the words represent states of consciousness**

Using the above suggestions in the order presented, here are interpretations for each word and phrase identified in STEP TWO:

Nouns:

   people—*MBD*, p. 513, "Our thoughts." The nature of people is reflected in their thoughts.

   little children—If people generally represent thoughts, then little children would represent thoughts of a pure, undefiled, unmodified nature.

   disciples—*MBD*, p. 175, "The disciples of Jesus represent, in mind analysis, the faculties. . . . The various faculties of the mind have been occupied almost wholly in secular ways; now they are to be turned to spiritual ways. . . . Truth reveals to us that every faculty must be used to spiritual ends in order that the law of Being may be fulfilled." *Strong's Concordance Greek Dictionary*, No. *3101*: μαθητής, transliterates as, MATHETES, meaning learner, pupil, disciple.

   Jesus—*MBD*, p. 345, "The *I* in man, the self, the directive power, raised to divine understanding and power—the I AM identity. Jesus represents God's idea of man in expression." *MBD*, p. 346, "Jesus' going about all the cities and villages, teaching, preaching, and healing, represents the I AM in its universal capacity as a teacher and harmonizer of its own mental and bodily conditions."

kingdom—*MBD*, p. 387, "The kingdom of heaven [God] is the orderly adjustment of divine ideas in man's mind and body." *MBD*, p. 388, "Jesus used many commonplace things to illustrate the establishing of the kingdom of heaven in consciousness in order that we might the more easily adjust all our thoughts and acts in harmony with the ideas that make heaven."

Verbs:

bringing—*Strong's Concordance's Greek Dictionary*, No. *4374*, προσφέρω, transliterates as PROSPHERO, meaning to bear towards, lead to, tender, bring, deal with, do, offer, present unto, put to.

touch—*Strong's Concordance's Greek Dictionary*, No. *680*, ἅπτομαι, transliterates as, HAPTOMAI, meaning attach oneself to, to touch. Metaphysically, to make conscious contact with a state of consciousness.

spoke sternly—*Strong's Concordance's Greek Dictionary*, No. *2008*, ἐπιτιμάω, transliterates as EPITIMAO, meaning to tax upon, censure, admonish, forbid, charge, rebuke. Metaphysically, to deny the power or importance of.

indignant—*Strong's Concordance's Greek Dictionary*, No. *23*, ἀγανακτέω, transliterates as AGANAKTEO, meaning to be greatly afflicted, indignant, much displeased. From ἄγαν (AGAN), meaning much, and ἄχθος (ACHTHOS), meaning indignation. Metaphysically, our natural dislike in response to the misguided actions of others.

tell—*Strong's Concordance's Greek Dictionary*, No. *3004*, λέγω, transliterates as LEGO, meaning to say forth, relate, ask, bid, boast, call, describe, give out, name, put forth, say, shew, speak, tell, utter.

receive—*Strong's Concordance's Greek Dictionary,* No. *1209,* δέχομαι, transliterates as DECHOMAI, meaning to accept, receive, take.

enter—*Strong's Concordance's Greek Dictionary,* No. *1525,* εἰσέρχομαι, transliterates as EISERCHOMAI, meaning to enter, arise, come in, go in.

took—*Strong's Concordance's Greek Dictionary,* No. *1723,* ἐναγκαλίζομαι, transliterates as ENAGKALIZOMAI, meaning to take in one's arms, embrace.

blessed—*Strong's Concordance's Greek Dictionary,* No. *2127,* εὐλογέω, transliterates as EULOGEO, meaning to speak well of, bless, thank, invoke a benediction upon, prosper, praise.

Other words and phrases:

stop—To hinder or get in the way of.

truly—*Strong's Concordance's Greek Dictionary,* No. *281,* ἀμήν, transliterates as AMEN, meaning firm, trustworthy, surely, so be it, verily.

never—This word has an air of finality about it.

STEP FOUR: ALLOW THE METAPHYSICAL MEANING TO EMERGE

- **Study, pray, and meditate on the overall story and the individual words interpreted in STEP THREE.**
- **Consult metaphysical interpretation books that interpret the selected passage(s):** Charles Fillmore's book *Keep a True Lent:*

> "Jesus said that before we can enter the kingdom of the heavens we must become as little children. Most children are bubbling over with happi-

ness. They have not yet been taught how to take life in the serious, solemn manner of the average adult. They hop and they skip and they sing, and their daily needs are met.

We all look back on the joys and freedom of our childhood and wish that they might have lasted always. And why not?

We have been taught that in mature life we have many hard lessons to learn, that trials and tribulations are an essential part of man's life, and that we must experience them in order to develop our character; that is, our consciousness. But Jesus said we must become as little children before we can enter the kingdom of heaven and that the kingdom is within us.

The little child has no consciousness of the tribulations of life, and the logical conclusion is that when we unload false states of mind and become childlike we shall begin to realize what heaven is like."[14]

- **Think about how these states of consciousness might correspond to events in your own life (i.e., healing of illness, conquering financial problems, dealing with persecution, overwhelming sense of joy, etc.):** This story propels me into my daily interactions with my own children. There are times when I behave like the disciples and want my children to stay out of my way because of my own grouchiness or fatigue. Other times I am more spiritually attuned, well-rested, cheerful, and very willing to "let the little children come to me." My attitude, not my children's, is the key to having a pleasant experience.
- **Utilize the many interpretive lenses (i.e., factual, historical, dramatic, comedic, etc.):** There was a moment of

drama in this story when Jesus' indignation created tension between him and the disciples. This tension added importance to the teaching that Jesus presented about the kingdom of God. We might also wonder about how the children felt when the disciples initially rebuffed them.

Morally speaking, this story emphasizes the spiritual value of children. They are not to be kept away out of sight but are to be included as much as possible in the arena of life, if not made the focus of life itself.

- **Explore common metaphysical themes (i.e., illumination, healing, prosperity, etc.) as they might apply:** Spiritual illumination takes place upon entering the kingdom of God. The wide-open honesty of children gives them the capacity to easily grasp spiritual ideas.
- **Apply your own innate creative intelligence—look at the story from many vantage points and perspectives:** One group not mentioned by name in the story are the parents of the children. The text generally refers to "people" bringing the children to Jesus. These "people" were probably their parents. One can imagine their excitement at having their children meet Jesus. Surely they were disappointed to see their children turned away by the disciples but relieved when Jesus called them over.
- **Remember, the metaphysical interpretive lens has an allegorical, psychological, and spiritual dimension:** This teaching of Jesus is highly metaphysical. First, Jesus uses the allegory of children by saying that we must "receive the kingdom of God as a little child" or we will "never enter it." We don't become a little child, for that is impossible. Instead, we receive the kingdom "as a little child." The key word is *as*; that is, we adopt the psychological openness and wonder of a child and leave behind our adult sophistication. Secondly,

Jesus once said, "The kingdom of God is within you."[15] So, we understand that the kingdom of God is not a nation in the heavens someplace where God sits on a throne but a spiritual state of consciousness.

- **Finally, ask yourself what jumps out at you about the passage? What clicks in you when you read it? Look for the personal, spiritual dimension that rises to the surface of your mind:** *Simplicity* is the word that jumps out at me when I read this story. Spiritual enlightenment does not require a Ph.D. If we are open, willing, receptive, and responsive to God, we enter God's kingdom. Nothing else is required. The simplest prayers and affirmations are always the best. Our minds easily grasp simplicity. Somewhere during the course of our lives we adopted the idea that spiritual Truth must be difficult or complex. This story says to me that we have to dump our intellectual concepts and superiority or we'll never experience the fullness of God.

- **Write down your interpretation as soon as it is revealed to you:** We read in the story that people (general realm of thoughts) presented little children (pure thoughts) to Jesus (I AM identity) so that he could touch (make contact with) them. It is out of the realm of thoughts (people) that pure thoughts (little children) emerge. The disciples (mental faculties), operating out of spiritual ignorance, spoke sternly (denied the importance) of these little children (pure thoughts) to the people (general realm of thought). Jesus (I AM presence) intervened with power and feeling (indignation). With firmness (truly) Jesus (I AM in its universal capacity as a teacher and harmonizer) told (lays forth) the disciples (mental faculties) that one will never enter (experience) the kingdom of God (divine ideas) until one takes into one's arms (embraces) little children (pure thoughts). Jesus (I AM presence) draws to him little children (pure thoughts) and blesses (prospers or enriches) them.

Summary

The Bible has been ingrained in the psyche of the Western world for thousands of years. Its characters and stories are archetypal. It is within our power to relate biblical material to our own spiritual journey and growth. We become Martha or Mary. We internally experience Jesus touching the children. The story of the Bible is the story of our lives, both outwardly and inwardly.

Also let me strongly emphasize that *there is more than one interpretation for the same biblical passage.* The sample interpretation put forth in this chapter is simply one person's view of the story of Jesus and the children. (See Appendix A for an Old Testament sample). Your interpretation will likely differ from mine in some fashion, if not significantly. The pivotal factor in any interpretation of the Bible is the individual mind of the interpreter. In a universal sense, there are virtually as many other interpretations as there are interpreters—that is, billions!

It is my hope, especially for those who are new to or unfamiliar with metaphysical Christianity, that this chapter has helped you to see the uniqueness and legitimacy of metaphysical Bible interpretation. The spiritual blessings and insights that result from metaphysical Bible study are what makes the Bible relevant to metaphysical Christians. No longer do the words *Bible study* mean we're in for a boring time. With the metaphysical interpretive lens in place, anyone can gaze upon the Bible with positive expectancy and harvest its spiritual potential.

Notes

1. During the writing of this book, Deepak Chopra was interviewed on CNN's *Larry King Live,* 8/22/95.

2. Genesis 1:26–27.

3. John 10:30–39.

4. The law of mind action is the law of cause and effect applied to human consciousness and experience.

5. Job 22:28.

6. Proverbs 23:7, KJV.

7. Matthew 7:7–8.

8. Job 3:25–26.

9. The author of this book is unknown. He was probably an English mystic living in the fourteenth century, since he wrote in the Middle English of that time period.

10. William Johnston (ed.), *The Cloud of Unknowing* (Garden City, New York: Image Books, 1973), pp. 71–72.

11. Isaiah 9:6, KJV.

12. Recall these words from George Frideric Handel's famous musical oratorio, *The Messiah.*

13. Included in most computer Bible programs.

14. Charles Fillmore, *Keep a True Lent* (Unity Village, Mo.: Unity Books, 1995), pp. 107–108.

15. Luke 17:21, KJV.

Chapter 10

Obtaining the Most From Your Bible

W*isdom for a Lifetime* could easily end with the ninth chapter, having adequately prepared the novice Bible student with the tools needed for deriving interesting, relevant, spiritual information from the Bible. However, I would be remiss if I did not suggest some different ways of thinking about the Bible that have enhanced my understanding of scripture. These ideas may help you fine-tune your interpretation of the Bible.

Modernizing the Bible

One of the biggest problems in reading the Bible is that the events took place in an era far removed from our own. The distance of time has reduced the Bible's relevancy in the minds of most people. This is understandable. It is difficult for modern people to relate to the lifestyle of those who lived some 2000–4000 years ago.[1] There are not very many people today living in technologically advanced countries who tend sheep for a living or drive chariots to work. However, there is a way to improve the relevancy of the Bible, to make it appear more real to us. We accomplish this by modernizing the story.

Imagine that the biblical story you are reading actually took place in your own time. Instead of projecting yourself back into the ancient story, as we often do in Bible study, bring the ancient figures forward to today as if they lived right next door. In modernizing the story, we use aspects and character-istics of our own time to update the people, places, objects, and language. This helps to make the biblical story appear more real and less a legend of the distant past. Consider this possible modernization of Luke 2:42–52, the story of the twelve-year-old Jesus in the Temple:

> Joseph, Mary, Jesus, and other family members have finished attending a family retreat at Unity Village, Missouri. In the busyness of getting into air-port shuttle buses, Jesus slips away to discuss deep spiritual truths with faculty members from the Unity School for Religious Studies.
>
> Two hours later Joseph and Mary are about to board the plane at Kansas City International for the trip back home to Nazareth, Pennsylvania, when they suddenly notice that Jesus is missing. Frantically, they leave the gate and make their way to a white courtesy telephone in hopes of paging and locating their lost son. After an hour of searching each of the three terminal buildings, they hop on the nearest de-parting rental car bus. Panic has begun to set in.
>
> After two sleepless and frantic days and nights and with all the law enforcement agencies of Western Missouri and Eastern Kansas aiding in their search, they are unable to find Jesus. Fearing the worst, and as a last resort, they drive to the Unity Village Peace Chapel to pray for God's guidance and assistance. As they approach the Chapel, Jesus casu-ally strides up to them.
>
> "Just where have you been? We've been looking all over for you," Joseph and Mary say in emphatic unison.

Joseph continues the cross-examination: "Your mother and I have been worried sick about you. Will you just look at her! The doctor had to give her a sedative, and my ulcer's been acting up. We've been to the police, highway patrol, you name it! Your picture has been on the evening news and is scheduled to be printed on some milk cartons. Do you have any idea what an ordeal you have put us through?"

Jesus stands and listens patiently without responding.

"That's it, you're grounded for the next week, and no video games for a month. Is that understood, young man?" adds Joseph.

Jesus calmly replies, "Relax, Mom and Dad. Chill out. I know you've probably been worried about me and all, but I figured I'd catch a later flight. Hey, you wouldn't believe what a wonderful place this is. I've met some very cool and intelligent people here, and guess what, they think I know my Truth pretty well too. Gee, I'd be willing to give up video games for a year to spend an extra day or two here at Unity Village. Didn't you parental types know that I'd be about my Father's business? Me and God, we've been busy!"

Joseph's face turns a beet red, then he threatens: "Speaking of your father's business, I've taken three extra vacation days off from my job at the furniture store looking for you. Don't push your luck, Son, or you will be giving up video games for a *year*!"

Now it's Mary's turn: "Jesus, come here, Son, and let me see you. When was the last time you ate, dear, you look hungry? Let's go to the Unity Inn and get some good food in you. You must be starving."

Joseph shakes his head in disbelief, "How can you possibly think of food at a time like this?" However, he follows behind Mary and Jesus, wondering what sort of surprise his son will pull on them next.

When you modernize a story, embellish it enough to make it feel as up-to-date as possible. Have fun while you're doing it.

"For the grace of God has appeared, bringing salvation to all."

—Titus 2:11

Let your creativity run loose. For example, when Jesus called Matthew as one of his disciples, he wasn't redeeming merely a tax collector but an IRS agent.[2] Somehow the words *IRS agent* evoke a more formidable and serious response in us than the rather dull, generic term *tax collector*.

There are books that can help you in this modernization process. Two of the better ones are *Olde Charlie Farquharson's Testament* and *Dick Gregory's Bible Tales*. These books have a way of lifting the Bible into a humorous yet decidedly more readable presentation. Here is a brief description of the books along with a sample from each.

Olde Charlie Farquharson's Testament is a down-on-the-farm, hayseed rendition of the Old Testament books of Genesis through Job, Daniel, Jonah, Psalms, Proverbs, Ecclesiastes, and the Song of Solomon. One of the first things you will notice is that these familiar Old Testament books have new names, such as Jennysez (Genesis), Exxodust (Exodus), and Due to Run on Me (Deuteronomy).

Jennysez 1:1–5 reads:

> At the start there wasn't a thing. That'd be yer Void. Dark too. Absoloot kayoss. So God decided to do something about it. He sed, Let's have some Light here. And there was. Right off. But there still weren't nothing to look at. He kept yer Dark too. Now he had two things going fer Him. Night and Day. He had the one foller the other so's He could keep track. That was all in one day's work.[3]

Dick Gregory's Bible Tales are a collection of Old and New Testament stories retold in a present-day manner with modern titles. Some of these titles include "The Cain Mutiny" (Genesis 4:1–16), "Up the River and Into a Foster Home" (Exodus 1:8—2:10), and "There Goes the Neighborhood" (Luke 10:25–37). Each story also includes a practical, contemporary, spiritual commentary.

Consider this description of John the Baptist from Chapter 23:

> In those days, there came a man known as John the Baptist. John was a rugged country preacher, who hung out in the wilderness and wore camel's-hair clothes. Unlike country preachers today, who have a fondness for fried chicken, John ate locusts and wild honey.[4]

Not every story can be successfully modernized. For example, read 1 Kings 3:16–28. With the use of electronic monitoring devices and other security measures, it is nearly impossible for someone to switch newborn babies in a hospital nursery. Even if the babies were not born in a hospital but at home, it is also unlikely that any persons involved in such a crime would appear together before a judge. Blood and DNA tests would be performed on the mothers and the babies to determine the correct parentage of the living one. Modernization does not work well in this instance, although it is interesting to explore. Fortunately for Solomon, his famous rendering, "divide the living boy in two; then give half to the one, and half to the other," will remain forever in the annals of judicial history (1 Kings 3:25). However, most stories can be modernized with a little creative thinking. Modernizing any story, biblical or not, can transform a musty, old tale into a modern-day occurrence to which almost anyone can relate. When a story becomes interesting, it is pretty difficult to resist reading.

Bible Wheat and Chaff

In the 1980s Wendy's restaurants ran television commercials portraying an elderly woman as a hamburger expert. Whenever she was presented with one of the competition's smaller burgers, she would loudly say, "Where's the beef?" Bible interpretation is often a matter of asking the same question. Where's the beef in the scripture? Some of it may seem like mostly bun. Where's the spiritual meaning in the many biblical genealogical lists? What positive, practical message is there for us in the depressing, gut-wrenching, tearful words of the book of Lamentations (which describes in great detail the miserable state of Jerusalem because of her sins)?

> **"Now faith is the assurance of things hoped for, the conviction of things not seen."**
>
> —Hebrews 11:1

In the Lord's Prayer, Jesus states, "Give us this day our daily bread."[5] The Bible can become a part of our daily spiritual bread, but not necessarily the *whole* Bible. You may find parts of the Bible and even entire books uninspiring and irrelevant. Laboriously reading these sections of the Bible is the leading cause of Bible apathy among metaphysical Christians. As I have stated, if a book is not readable nor relevant, we usually don't bother reading it. We are attracted to subjects in which we have an interest. Interest translates into an energy that results in reading and studying.

Separating the wheat from the chaff, the usable and interesting from the impractical and boring, is one of your jobs as a Bible student. Just because something is in the Bible does not necessarily make it worth reading or interpreting. If the ultimate purpose of Bible study is to uncover practical, life-transformative meaning from the Bible, then we must discern what is wheat and what is not. This is accomplished through the use of the literary interpretive lens introduced in Chapter 8. Learn to use discretion when reading the Bible. Become your own biblical, literary critic. If you don't, I guarantee the chaff of the Bible will catapult you toward greener literary pastures.

Being your own biblical, literary critic means you must keep your eyes open for the wheat and be able to disregard the chaff. Look for those passages and stories that stir your soul. We might call this kind of sight "sacred gaze." Chapter 3 made reference to the sacred quality of the world's scriptures. Sacredness is not something determined by ecclesiastical organizations. What makes the Bible personally sacred to us has to do

> **"But the wisdom from above is first pure, then peaceable, gentle, willing to yield, full of mercy and good fruits, without a trace of partiality or hypocrisy."**
> —James 3:17

with the way our souls respond to it—whether we read it during our devotional time or hear it read in church. It is the wheat of the Bible that feeds our souls, that awakens our awareness to a deeper level. Any book that feeds our souls is sacred. The chaff of the Bible doesn't need to be sacred or holy just because it is in the Bible. So don't fret over those parts of the Bible that appear spiritually inert. Let them be as straw on a threshing room floor to be used for less important purposes. Later you may wish to sweep up some of the chaff and explore its spiritual potential. Remember, the Truth we see is based upon what is relevant to us. We tend to identify with and be drawn to those stories and passages that relate most to what is going on in our lives at any given time. Relevancy changes with the passing of time. What we once saw as chaff can become wheat—or beef if you have a hankering for a Wendy's hamburger.

Questioning Scripture

Have you ever read a book that you initially considered to be authoritative only to later question or even disagree with its content? This personal critique of literature also applies to reading the Bible. For literal Bible students afflicted with the "God-wrote-it-and-that's-the-end-of-it syndrome," this concept is positively sacrilegious.

However, just because something is written in the Bible does not mean we have to wholeheartedly embrace it. It has been stated that scriptures become sacred to us because of the way our souls respond to their words. The same can be said of their authority as well. This takes us a step beyond simply separating the wheat from the chaff to determining that some of the chaff we have set aside is totally useless and perhaps even detrimental to our spiritual well-being.

This stance may appear to be un-Christian. How dare we say that the Bible in any way lacks authority in our lives? The key words here are *in any way.* As Christians, it is unreasonable to demand that we have to buy everything written in the Bible. Many statements in the Bible may not only fail to hit home with us, but some may directly conflict with our personal, spiritual beliefs. Even if we had lived, for instance, in the time of the Old Testament prophets, would we have necessarily agreed with their exhortations to change our ways? Not many did. Today do you agree with every modern spiritual book you read? I doubt it. Most progressive and metaphysical Christians do not accept the infallible authority of the Bible.

It is you, the Bible student, who must judge the veracity and authority of the scriptures for yourself and not someone else. To question the Bible is not to show disrespect for it but to prayerfully discern its value. Fundamentalist Christians supposedly ascribe authority to the whole Bible. However, even these well-meaning Bible students could not possibly practice *all* the Bible suggests. To accept the entire Bible as authority is to become like the Pharisees of Jesus' day who tried and failed to follow the hundreds of religious statutes required of their brand of Judaism. Therefore, prayerfully select those passages from the Bible that call forth the highest and best in you. Give them the weight of authority in your own heart. If you happen to disagree with what you read, it is okay! You have my permission! It is difficult to determine whether or not something in the Bible happened because we were not there to witness the event. However, we can disagree with the conclusions of the biblical writers if that is our guidance.

You may, for instance, object to this legal statute spelled out in the book of Leviticus: "Anyone who maims another shall suffer the same injury in return: fracture for fracture, eye for eye, tooth for tooth; the injury inflicted is the injury to be suffered."[6] Most civilized people would find this practice barbaric, and yet it is in the Bible.

Consider Paul's first letter to the Corinthians. Contained within this document are some of the finest passages in the Bible. In Chapter 12, Paul clearly outlines the diversity of spiritual gifts among people as well as the Spirit that unites them. Chapter 13 is perhaps the most beautiful love literature ever written. However, there are chapters of 1 Corinthians that contain ideas which are offensive to many Christians.

In Chapters 5–6, Paul sternly admonishes the Corinthian church after receiving reports of their immoral behavior. He writes:

> "Do you now know that the wicked will not inherit the kingdom of God? Do not be deceived: Neither the sexually immoral nor idolaters nor adulterers nor male prostitutes nor homosexual offenders nor thieves nor the greedy nor drunkards nor slanderers nor swindlers will inherit the kingdom of God."[7]

Our modern society is made of people who, according to Paul's definitions, would be considered to be immoral and thus cut off from the kingdom of God. Certainly no well-adjusted, sane person would endorse adultery, stealing, prostitution, alcoholism, or chicanery as socially acceptable, moral behavior.

These acts cause immense harm and need to be renounced, as Paul suggests. However, to include homosexuals in this category is outrageous to many Christians.

Along a similar line, how many women today would agree with this viewpoint from Chapter 14:

> "As in all congregations of God's people, women should not address the meeting. They have no licence to speak, but should keep their place as the law directs. If there is something they want to know, they can ask their own husbands at home. It is a shocking thing that a woman should address the congregation."[8]

I deliberately chose the NEB for this quote because its language is least offensive to women. Other English translations refer to women speaking in church as being disgraceful or shameful. I would venture to say that most women, upon reading this part of 1 Corinthians would like to tell Paul where to go . . . perhaps off a cliff! Just within the Unity movement alone, there are over five hundred women ministers, one of whom sits at the head of Unity School of Christianity.[9] Paul has labeled them as shocking, if not deplorable.

Paul is a problem for most metaphysical Christians. On one hand, he has some marvelous thoughts,[10] and on the other, he seems to be living on another planet. Paul wrote these letters to offer advice and counsel to the churches in much the same way a denominational leader would today. His recommendations reflect his bias, era, culture, and world view. Do his ideas transfer to modern times? That is for you to decide. If you want to disagree with Paul, it does not make you any less a Christian. Whenever possible, glean what good you can from him and try not to be too offended by his narrow-mindedness. Realize that other people may agree with what you object to.

Whether it is Paul or another biblical writer, keep in mind that what we interpret from the passage may not be the original intent of the author. In most cases, the original intent of the author has to do with the context in which the author is writing. Remember, the Bible was written by human beings like ourselves. Their written words reflect their personal opinions and were intended for the people of their time. To some extent, any present-day reading of the Bible is done out of context simply because we are so far removed from the era of the biblical events. It is extremely presumptuous of us to think that they were writing for our benefit, although we do benefit from their efforts.

To understand original intent, we must ask some basic questions:

(1) Who were the authors?

(2) To whom is the writing directed?

(3) What is the likely underlying motivation for the writing?

(4) What message did the writers intend for their audience to comprehend?

These questions are very different from those we ask to interpret the Bible for our own personal growth and understanding. However, asking and answering these questions will help you gain historical balance and understanding regarding those challenging Bible passages. Bible commentaries are particularly useful in ascertaining original intent.

One way of dealing with disturbing or puzzling Bible passages is to consult other versions (see Chapter 5 for a list of translations). Another translation can add a whole new dimension to a difficult verse. For many years the line from the Lord's Prayer, "lead us not into temptation," bothered me. I wondered how a loving, merciful God could lead or not lead anyone into an experience that wasn't for his or her highest good? Finally, I consulted several other translations of the Lord's Prayer and found the Phillips Modern English rendering, "keep us clear of temptation," much more acceptable. What a change. My concept of God remained intact as I prayed this prayer anew. For me, God is the power that keeps me clear of temptation.

Most of us either own or have seen a red-letter edition of the Bible in which Jesus' words are printed in red. Imagine a Bible where Jesus' words are printed in red, pink, gray, and black. Questioning the veracity of scripture is not just reserved for metaphysically oriented people. In 1985 a group of scholars, known as the Jesus Seminar, began a quest for the historical Jesus. Over a period of six years, these scholars asked and answered the question, "What did Jesus really say?"[11] The result of their effort was a book entitled *The Five Gospels,* featuring a fresh translation of The Gospels known as the Scholars Version (SV).[12] Throughout *The Five Gospels,* Jesus' words appear in different colors indicating the authenticity the scholars gave to them.

> **"You have been born anew, not of perishable but of imperishable seed, through the living and enduring word of God."**
> —1 Peter 1:23

Questioning the words of Paul or the Hebrew Bible may be a radical idea in many Christian circles but challenging the words of Jesus is tantamount to blasphemy. Sometimes it takes a little blasphemy to reveal a new and perhaps a more enlightened way of looking at long-treasured beliefs and concepts. If you are interested in evaluating Jesus' words, *The Five Gospels* is definitely worth considering.

Yet in reading any version of the Bible, if you stumble upon a Bible passage that turns you off, do not summarily dismiss it. Take a stab at interpreting it. Redeeming value can be found in even the least endearing verse. For example:

> "And everyone who utters a word against the son of Adam, will be forgiven; but whoever blasphemes against the holy spirit won't be forgiven."—Luke 12:10, SV

This statement of Jesus has always unnerved me. It is the basis for the concept, The Unpardonable Sin, something which traditional Christians have been fearful of for centuries. Given that Jesus' basic message was one of love and forgiveness, it seems inconsistent that there could be any unforgivable sins. After all, are not sins and mistakes the very thing forgiveness transforms?

When we reject the influence of the Holy Spirit in our lives, we mentally cut ourselves off from the very source of the life that moves in and through us. Divine potential is trying to express but is hampered through our obstinate attitude. We are in what might be called an *unforgiven state.* The longer we remain in this state of consciousness, the more alone, isolated, and unforgiven we feel.

This *unforgiven state* is not permanent. The moment we let go of our obstinacy, we immediately experience an inflow of the Holy Spirit and are restored to our natural state of spiritual wholeness. We realize the importance of being willing to let God's spirit work *through* us rather than bouncing off us.

It is noteworthy that Luke 12:10 appears in the Jesus Seminar's Scholars Version as black, as words that Jesus did not likely say. This verse may have come from a later or different tradition.

Thematic Bible Interpretation

Most metaphysical Christians, depending upon their individual needs, often focus their attention on specific topics such as divine order, enlightenment, guidance, healing, inner peace, prosperity, protection, relationships, and so forth. A better understanding and application of these teachings in one's life can be enhanced by biblical study. When we read the Bible through the interpretive lens of one of these subjects, we are employing thematic Bible interpretation, introduced in Chapter 9.

Excellent examples of thematic Bible interpretation can be found in the writings of Catherine Ponder and Georgiana Tree

West, mentioned in Chapter 4. These writers wrote their interpretations of scripture through the interpretive lens of prosperity. What appeared as simple Bible stories to others became prosperity lessons in their eyes.

For instance, the character of Abraham in the Old Testament is ordinarily considered to be the man whose covenant with God established him as the father and founder of the Hebrew people. Metaphysically, Abraham represents the awakening of faith.[13] Nevertheless, did you ever think of him as the first millionaire of the Bible?

> **"There is no fear in love, but perfect love casts out fear."**
>
> —1 John 4:18

He was. When we look at the events of his life through the interpretive lens of prosperity, we see a pattern of prosperous acts emerge. Allow me to demonstrate.

(1) Read Genesis 12:1–5. It took a great deal of faith for Abraham to leave his hometown and travel to a faraway land. In order for us to prosper, we have to be willing to take risks and step out on faith into unknown territory, whether it's marketing a totally new product or moving to a distant city to accept a job promotion. Abraham followed his intuition and made the move to Canaan hundreds of miles from his home. He did this without the benefit of a moving company, air-conditioned cars, and rest areas every hundred miles. **Abraham established his faith in God.**

(2) Read Genesis 12:16—13:2. Abraham went into Egypt and returned with livestock, slaves, gold, and silver. He was rich, a real tycoon. Metaphysically, Egypt represents the realm of substance and material consciousness.[14] If we wish to experience abundance, in essence, we have to spend time in Egypt. In other words, we must open to the good of the material world and not reject it as too secular or profane. **Abraham accepted his good without hesitation.**

(3) Read Genesis 13:8–12. Abraham was so secure in his own prosperity that he gave his nephew Lot whatever land he wanted. He knew the Truth that his good could never be taken

from him. We are required by society to be responsible, to meet our financial obligations in a timely manner. How often do we give when it is not demanded of us? Abraham did not have to give Lot his pick of the land, but he did, and yet he continued to prosper. **Abraham gave when it was not required.**

(4) Read Genesis 14:18-20. Melchizedek, the king and priest of Salem, blessed Abraham with positive words and re-freshment. Afterward, Abraham tithed to him. When we tithe, we are participating in the law of circulation. Tithing is the most effective way of giving to support spiritual organizations for present and future generations. Jesus said, "Give, and it will be given to you."[15] In return for participating in this law, we receive whatever good we need. **Abraham tithed to the channel of his spiritual good.**

(5) Read Genesis 18:23–33. Abraham interceded on behalf of Sodom and Gomorrah to save them from destruction. The text reveals that Abraham was a masterful negotiator. How he was able to talk God down to just ten righteous men is a feat unmatched by any professional negotiator since. This story demonstrates that giving involves more than money. Like Abraham, we can share our unique tal-ents and abilities to help others. It is unfortunate for Sodom and Gomorrah that ten righteous men could not be found, but that was their problem. Abraham did his best. That's all we can do. People have to help themselves too. **Abraham gave of his time and talent to help others.**

"Let us love one another."
—2 John 1:5

(6) Read Genesis 22:9–14. Isaac's birth was a miracle, a demonstration of prosperity for Abraham and Sarah. However, Abraham was moved to take his son up a mountain and sacri-fice him.[16] Fortunately for Isaac, just as his father was plunging the knife toward him, an angel halted his advance, and Abraham spotted a ram in a nearby thicket. Abraham named the place, Jehovah-Jireh, or "The Lord will provide." We, too, are put to the test by the circumstances of life. When it seems there is no

other way to provide for ourselves other than to sacrifice our values and principles, our ram shows up in the thicket and we are provided with exactly what we need. Our faith in God as the one source is reaffirmed. **Abraham had a consciousness that the Lord will provide.**

As you can see, Abraham was indeed the Bible's first millionaire. There is much we can learn about our own experience of prosperity by observing his life through the *lens of prosperity.* Try your hand at thematic interpretation. Become observant of the actions and results of the Bible characters. Look for any consistent patterns. Experiment with it a bit. Remember, it is your mind set, the interpretive lens that you are looking through, that draws out the desired teaching from the Bible. As with any interpretive lenses, not all Bible stories will conform to your theme, but you'll be surprised by how many will.

Bible Study Tips

READING THE BIBLE FROM COVER TO COVER. Every year there is a road race in San Francisco called Bay to Breakers. The purpose of the race is to run as fast as you can from the bay side of the city on the east to the ocean beaches on the west, a total of about eight miles. Whenever we read a book, we nearly always read it in its entirety starting with the first page. Because of this practice, there is a natural inclination for us to read through the Bible as if it were any other book. If you read the Bible from cover to cover, do so quickly at first, as if you were running the Bay to Breakers race. Avoid being bogged down in the more tedious parts. Let them go by as quickly passing scenery. Remember your purpose is to quickly take in the Bible's words. As you encounter interesting passages, make a note of them for further in-depth study at a later time.

READ A CONDENSED BIBLE. Another way of reading the Bible all the way through is to read a condensed version of the Bible. *Reader's Digest* is famous for its condensed books, including the Bible (see Chapter 5). This approach will allow you to read the Bible as if it were a singular book. Always remember that a condensed Bible is not an accurate translation but a paraphrase.

TAKE COURSES IN BIBLE STUDY. Your local church, college, or seminary probably offers classes in Bible study. Unity School of Christianity teaches courses in Bible history and interpretation at its world headquarters at Unity Village, Missouri, and at regionally sponsored sessions.

READ THE BIBLE DEVOTIONALLY. Read the Bible as a part of your daily devotional practice.

MEDITATE ON BIBLE VERSES. Use short, positive Bible verses as your theme for meditation.

JOIN A BIBLE STUDY GROUP. Get together with other like-minded people, and pool your creative genius in studying the Bible.

READ THE MOTEL BIBLE. When was the last time you actually read the motel Bible? It's in the drawer by the bedside lamp. Fan through it a few times. Do a little trolling. Read whatever page your finger lands on.

PLAY BIBLE GAMES. Computer and board games are available that pertain to the Bible. These test your Bible knowledge.

GO ON-LINE WITH THE BIBLE. The Bible has made its way on to the Internet. On-line computer services (that is America Online, CompuServe, Prodigy, and so forth) have topic folders and forums where you can talk with other interested people about the Bible. Entire biblical libraries are also available.

Summary

After completing this book, you may begin to sense just how immense and complex the Bible actually is. You may feel overwhelmed by the task of Bible study and underqualified to do justice to it. Don't worry about it. Set your lack of Bible acumen and confidence aside and study what you can, and more important, what interests you. You don't have to be a scholar to read the Bible, but you do have to be motivated to unearth its treasure. Hopefully, this book has equipped you sufficiently to gain useful, personally relevant spiritual ideas from biblical study. Don't sweat it. Follow your nose. Obtain whatever good you can. Let your biblical skills develop gradually. Whatever gains you make biblically accumulate over time. Do you recall how dusty your Bible used to be, stuck away on a bookshelf somewhere? Now it's on your reading stack. Soon it will be in your hands!

Please realize that you do not need to know everything about the Bible to get some good from it. It is highly unlikely that in the scope of your lifetime you will know all there is to know about the Bible. I would be the first person to admit that I do not know every story, detail, verse, or interpretation of the Bible. I know what I know, and I'm learning more. No one person knows everything there is to know about the Bible, not even trained Bible scholars. Take the pressure off yourself. Relax. You'll study all that much better if you do. Your task is not to know everything there is to know about the Bible, but to know what you need to know for your own spiritual growth.

Notes

1. From the time of Abraham and Sarah through the New Testament. Most scholars agree that Adam, Eve, Noah, and other pre-Patriarchal persons were symbolic figures rather than historical people.

2. Matthew 9:9–13.

3. Don Harron, *Olde Charlie Farquharson's Testament* (Toronto: Macmillan of Canada, 1978), p. 1.

4. Dick Gregory, *Dick Gregory's Bible Tales* (New York: Harper & Row, 1978), p. 152.

5. Matthew 6:11.

6. Leviticus 24:19–20.

7. 1 Corinthians 6:9–10, NIV.

8. 1 Corinthians 14:33–35, NEB.

9. Rev. Connie Fillmore Bazzy is the president of Unity School of Christianity.

10. One of Charles Fillmore's favorite verses was "Christ in you, the hope of glory" (Col. 1:27).

11. Robert W. Funk, Roy W. Hoover, and the Jesus Seminar, *The Five Gospels* (New York: Macmillan, 1993), p. ix.

12. The fifth gospel of the book is the Gospel of Thomas, originally written in Greek during the second century C.E. This book survives today in Coptic from the 1945 discovery of the Nag Hammadi library in Egypt. Although excluded from the Christian canon, the gospel of Thomas contains 114 statements attributed to Jesus, some of which seem to coincide with the synoptic gospels of Matthew, Mark, and Luke.

13. *Metaphysical Bible Dictionary* (Unity Village, Mo.: Unity Books, 1995), p. 18.

14. Ibid., p. 183.

15. Luke 6:38.

16. Human sacrifice was a part of Canaanite culture. Although the biblical text states that God directed Abraham to sacrifice Isaac, it is just as likely that he was following this ancient, barbaric custom. Or, as some scholars say, this story was included to explain the origin of the practice of offering the first-born son (later modified to dedicating the firstborn son to God's service). Also it may have been placed here to have the Hebrews substitute animals for human sacrifice.

Appendix A

Using the Four-Step Process of Metaphysical Bible Interpretation

The following is a systematic, thorough, metaphysical interpretation of a familiar Old Testament Bible story using the Four-Step Process. Each of the steps and suggested approaches has been included for easy reference and practical repetition.

STEP ONE: SELECT, READ, AND STUDY THE SCRIPTURE

- **Select the passage(s) to be studied:** Exodus 14:15–31— Crossing of the Red Sea by Moses and the Israelites. The New Revised Standard Version will be the translation used to select words for interpretation.
- **Read the passage(s) several times:**

  "Then the Lord said to Moses, 'Why do you cry out to me? Tell the Israelites to go forward. But you lift up your staff, and stretch out your hand over the sea and divide it, that the Israelites may go into the sea on dry ground. Then I will harden the hearts of the Egyptians so that they will go in after them; and so I will gain glory for myself over Pharaoh and all his army, his chariots, and his chariot drivers. And the Egyptians shall know that I am the Lord, when I have gained glory for myself over Pharaoh, his chariots, and his chariot drivers.' The angel of God who was going before the Israelite army moved and went behind them; and the pillar of cloud moved from in front of them and took its place behind them. It came between the army of Egypt and the army of Israel. And so the cloud was there with the darkness, and it lit up the night; one did not come near the other all night. Then Moses stretched out his hand over the sea. The Lord drove the sea back by a strong east wind all night, and turned the sea into dry land; and the waters were divided. The Israelites went into the sea on dry ground, the waters forming a wall for them on their right and on their left. The Egyptians pursued, and went into the sea after them, all of Pharaoh's horses, chariots, and chariot drivers. At the morning watch the Lord in the pillar of fire and cloud looked down upon the Egyptian army, and threw the Egyptian army into panic. He clogged their chariot wheels so that they turned with difficulty. The Egyptians said, 'Let us flee from the Israelites, for the Lord is fighting for them against Egypt.' Then the Lord said to Moses, 'Stretch out your hand over the sea, so that the water may come back upon the Egyptians, upon their chariots and chariot drivers.' So Moses stretched out his hand over the sea, and at dawn the sea returned to its normal depth. As the Egyptians fled before it, the Lord tossed the Egyptians into the sea. The waters returned and covered the chariots and the chariot drivers, the entire army of Pharaoh that had followed them into the sea; not one of them remained. But the Israelites walked on dry ground through the sea, the waters forming a wall for them on their right and on their left. Thus the Lord saved Israel that day from the

Egyptians; and Israel saw the Egyptians dead on the seashore. Israel saw the great work that the Lord did against the Egyptians. So the people feared the Lord and believed in the Lord and in his servant Moses."[1]

- **Consult a Bible dictionary for general information on distinctive or unfamiliar words:** Look up *Moses, Pharaoh, Egypt, chariot, sea (Red Sea)*.
- **Consult Bible commentaries and handbooks for historical and scholastic information on the biblical book, chapter, and verses:** Many scholars propose that the crossing of the water may not have been a supernatural event but could have occurred by the action of the winds and tides that quickly altered the water level.
- **Consult a Bible atlas to determine the location of the biblical event:** Atlases indicate that the crossing of the Red Sea, or the Sea of Reeds, could have taken place in a number of possible locations between Egypt and the Sinai Peninsula, including some marshes, bitter lakes, and swamps. None of these places can be verified with any degree of certainty as the crossing place.
- **Gain a basic understanding of the story line:** Moses and the Israelites, while escaping from the attacking Egyptian army, faced a body of water they must successfully cross to survive. The story is an account of how God's intervention made it possible for them to safely cross the water and prevented the Egyptians from further pursuit.

STEP TWO: IDENTIFY THE KEY WORDS AND PHRASES

- **Scan the passage for those verses and words that you feel are most important to the meaning of the story line or are unique in character, listed in the order they appear in the text.**
- **Nouns: proper names, people, places, objects, animals:** *Lord, Moses, Israelites, staff, hand, sea, Red Sea, dry*

ground, hearts, Egyptians, Egypt, Pharaoh, army, chariots, angel, God, pillar of cloud, strong east wind, waters, wall, pillar of fire, servant
- **Verbs: actions, movements, thoughts, feelings:** cry out, go forward, lift up, stretch out, divide, harden, pursued, clogged, returned, saved, feared, believed
- **Other words or phrases that are descriptive of the scene:** panic, difficulty, normal depth

STEP THREE: DEVELOP INTERPRETATIONS FOR THE WORDS

- **Consult the** *Metaphysical Bible Dictionary* **for suggested interpretations of proper names, name places, and special words (i.e.,** Moses, Israelites, sea, Red Sea, Egyptians, Egypt, Pharaoh, chariots, angel, waters**)**
- **Consult an English dictionary (such as** *Webster's Dictionary*) **and a thesaurus for the meaning of and synonyms for common words (i.e.,** Lord, staff, hand, dry ground, pillar of cloud, strong east wind, pillar of fire, servant, difficulty**)**
- **Use** *Strong's Concordance*'s **Hebrew and Greek dictionaries to obtain exegetical information on selected words**
- **Consider how the words represent states of consciousness**

Using the above suggestions in the order presented, here are interpretations for each word and phrase identified in STEP TWO:

Nouns:

Lord—Not found in *MBD*[2]. Another word for God in the Old Testament. *Strong's Concordance Hebrew Dictionary*, No. 3068: יהוה, which transliterates into English as YEHOVAH or YAHWEH, meaning the name of the Hebrew God, Supreme Being,

Self-existent. Among many Jews, this word is considered too holy to speak. It is usually translated into English as Lord. Metaphysically, it is the highest state of consciousness, pure, unmodified, without attributes, the spiritual nature of humankind.

Moses—*MBD,* p. 461: "Moses symbolizes this progressive or *drawing-out* process, which works from within outward; as applied to the universe, the upward trend of all things—the evolutionary law." *Strong's Concordance Hebrew Dictionary,* No. 4872: מֹשֶׁה, transliterates as MOSHEH, or Moses, meaning drawing out. Moses was drawn out by God to free the Israelites. The Israelites were drawn out of their servitude by Moses. Metaphysically, Moses is the activity of God that draws us upward and onward spiritually.

Israelites—*MBD,* pp. 304–05: "The illumined thoughts in consciousness, which are undergoing spiritual discipline. They are the total of our religious thoughts. In the beginning of our journey from sense consciousness to spiritual consciousness, from Egypt to the Promised Land, not all these religious thoughts are awake to spiritual Truth." *Strong's Concordance Hebrew Dictionary,* Nos. 1121 and 3478: בְּנֵי-יִשְׂרָאֵל, transliterates as BEN-ISRAEL, meaning sons or descendants of Israel—in other words, Israelites. Metaphysically, they are us, learning, growing, endeavoring to be free from bondage to negativity and materiality.

staff—*Webster's Dictionary:* A rod carried as a symbol of authority. Metaphysically, it is the authority of the word in affirming the Truth.

hand—*Webster's Dictionary:* Middle English derived from the Old English, akin to Gothic, *handus,* meaning, to deal with.

sea—*MBD,* p. 578: "We sometimes think of a 'sea,' too, as a state of unrest."

Red Sea—*MBD,* p. 549: "The Red Sea represents the sum of all the thoughts about life with which the race has impregnated the universal ether. In the mythology of the Greeks and the

Romans this is symbolized by the river Styx, over which souls were ferried by Charon. It is familiar to metaphysicians as the psychic realm or race thought, which has to be overcome by the progressive soul."

dry ground—*Webster's Dictionary:* basis or foundation. Metaphysically, consciousness free from the unrest of the waters or sea.

hearts—*Strong's Concordance Hebrew Dictionary*, No. 3820: לֵב, transliterates as LEB, meaning heart, but also used figuratively for the feelings, the will, and even the intellect.

Egyptians—*MBD*, p. 184: "Egyptians signify sense thoughts, or thoughts that pertain to the subjective consciousness in its unawakened state. They belong to the Egypt consciousness.

Egypt—*MBD*, p. 183: "Egypt signifies the darkness of ignorance, obscurity; it has a special significance in the body consciousness, and we often think of it as referring to the subjective or subconscious mind. We also refer to Egypt as the flesh consciousness, sense consciousness, or material consciousness."

Pharaoh—*MBD*, pp. 519–20: "Pharaoh means *the sun*. He is ruler of the solar plexus, the sun center in the subconscious mind. This is obscurity, or Egypt, to the conscious mind. Pharaoh's *(the sun's)* being in Egypt shows us that the light of the sun of righteousness is veiled by our life on the lower or sense plane. . . . Moses and Pharaoh represent two forces at work in the consciousness—especially that part pertaining to the body. Moses represents the evolutionary force of new ideas that have grown in the subconscious mind, that are tugging at the old states of limitation and material ignorance and trying to rise into a higher life expression. Pharaoh represents the force that rules the body under the material *régime.* The Lord (Jehovah, as given in the American Standard Version) is here the universal law, the impulse of which is always upward and onward, yet seeking always to preserve equilibrium."

army—*Strong's Concordance Hebrew Dictionary,* No. 2428: חיל, transliterates as CHAYIL, meaning force, whether of men, means, or other resources; an army, wealth, virtue, valor, strength.

chariots—*MBD,* p. 142: "Chariots, in the Bible, represent the body activities." *Strong's Concordance Hebrew Dictionary,* No. 7393: רכב, transliterates as REKEB, meaning vehicle. Also No. 7392: רכב, transliterated as RAKAB, meaning to ride, place upon, despatch. Metaphysically, chariots are the vehicles by which we traverse thought and feeling.

angel—*MBD,* p. 52: "Our angels are our spiritual perceptive faculties, which ever dwell in the presence of the Father. . . . The angel mentioned in Exodus 3:2 symbolizes a *messenger;* it is the projection into consciousness of a spiritual idea." *Strong's Concordance Hebrew Dictionary,* No. 4397: מלאך, transliterates as MALAK, meaning to despatch as a deputy, messenger, ambassador, king, priest, prophet, or teacher.

God—Not found in *MBD. Strong's Concordance Hebrew Dictionary,* No. 430: אלהים, transliterates as ELOHIYM, meaning gods, Supreme God.

pillar of cloud—Was the physical indication to the Israelites of God's presence during the day. Metaphysically, blocks negativity from awareness.

strong east wind—Metaphysically, east denotes an inner, spiritual direction. Hence the activity that opens the way for the Israelites comes from within and does so with strength and power.

waters—*MBD,* pp. 675–76: "Water in its different aspects represents weakness and negativeness, cleansing, mental potentiality, and in some cases life, or vital energy. . . . Water also represents the great mass of thoughts that conform to environment. Every thought leaves its form in the consciousness, and all the weak, characterless words and expressions gather in the subconscious mind as water gathers in holes. When we get discouraged or disappointed and give up, the undertow of life sweeps this flood of negative thought over us, and we are conscious of bodily weakness of some sort. Then, if we get scared, there is trouble ahead."

wall—*Strong's Concordance Hebrew Dictionary*, No. 2346: חומה, transliterates as CHOWMAH, meaning to join, a wall of protection. Metaphysically, a protective boundary in consciousness.

pillar of fire—Was the physical indication to the Israelites of God's presence during the night. Metaphysically, illumines awareness in consciousness.

servant—One who serves.

Verbs:

cry out—*Strong's Concordance Hebrew Dictionary*, No. 6817: צעק, transliterates as TSA'AQ, meaning to shriek, proclaim, cry out, gather.

go forward—*Strong's Concordance Hebrew Dictionary*, No. 5265: נסע, transliterates as NACA, meaning to pull up, start on a journey, cause to blow, bring, get, (make to) go (away, forth, forward, onward, out), be on his way.

lift up—*Strong's Concordance Hebrew Dictionary*, No. 7311: רום, transliterates as RUWM, meaning to be high, to rise or raise. Also, bring up, exalt, give.

stretch out—*Strong's Concordance Hebrew Dictionary*, No. 5186: נטה, transliterates as NATAH, meaning to stretch or spread out. Also, stretch forth, offer, intend, deliver, extend.

divide—*Strong's Concordance Hebrew Dictionary*, No. 1234: בקע, transliterates as BAQA, meaning to cleave, rend, break, rip, or open. Also, make a breach, break forth, cut out, divide, tear, win.

harden—*Strong's Concordance Hebrew Dictionary*, No. 2388: חזק, transliterates as CHAZAQ, meaning to fasten upon, seize, be strong, obstinate, bind, restrain, conquer. Also, force, harden, maintain, withstand.

pursued—*Strong's Concordance Hebrew Dictionary,* No. 7291: רדף, transliterates as RADAPH, meaning run after, chase, put to flight, follow, hunt, persecute, pursue.

clogged—*Strong's Concordance Hebrew Dictionary,* No. 5493: שׁוּר, transliterates as SUWR, meaning to turn off. Also, remove, take off, be without.

returned—*Strong's Concordance Hebrew Dictionary,* No. 7725: שׁוּב, transliterates as SHUWB, to turn back, return. Also, retreat, draw back, recall, withdraw.

saved—*Strong's Concordance Hebrew Dictionary,* No. 3467: ישׁע, transliterates as YASHA, meaning to be open, wide, free, safe. Also, defend, deliver, preserve, save, get victory.

feared—*Strong's Concordance Hebrew Dictionary,* No. 3372: ירא, transliterates as YARE, meaning to fear, revere.

believed—*Strong's Concordance Hebrew Dictionary,* No. 539: אמן, transliterates as AMAN, meaning to build up, support, foster, render, be firm, faithful, trust, believe.

Other words and phrases:

panic—*Strong's Concordance Hebrew Dictionary,* No. 2000: המם, transliterates as HAMAM, meaning to put in commotion, disturb, drive, destroy. Also, break, consume, discomfit, trouble, vex. Metaphysically, fear of annihilation.

difficulty—*Webster's Dictionary:* not easy, hard, trouble.

normal depth—*Strong's Concordance Hebrew Dictionary,* No. 386: איתן, transliterates as AYTHAN, meaning to continue, permanence.

STEP FOUR: ALLOW THE METAPHYSICAL MEANING TO EMERGE

- Study, pray, and meditate on the overall story and the individual words interpreted in STEP THREE.
- Consult metaphysical interpretation books that interpret the selected passage(s):

Elizabeth Sand Turner's book, *Let There Be Light:* "There comes a time when man makes his escape from the realm of the sense consciousness (represented by Egypt), but he is still far from being on a permanently spiritual level of activity. As Truth students we have left Egypt but have not reached the Promised Land."[3]

William Cameron's book, *Great Dramas of the Bible:*

> Then there were the incredible events of the Red Sea, in which the pharaoh thought the Hebrews would be stopped.
>
> A youngster once came home from his first Sunday school class at church and his father asked him to tell what he had learned. The boy said, "We learned about Moses crossing the Red Sea." The father said, "Tell me about it." The boy then said, "Moses was helping his people escape from Egypt and the pharaoh began to chase them in chariots. When the Hebrews got to the Red Sea, they built a pontoon bridge and crossed over. When the Egyptians began to cross the bridge, Moses got on his walkie-talkie, called in the artillery, and blew them up." His father said, "Did they tell you that?" The boy said, "Well, Dad, if you don't believe that, you would never believe what they did tell me."
>
> The spiritual importance of the Red Sea story is that it was the site of one of our most encouraging biblical truths: . . . *"Fear not, stand firm, and see the salvation of the Lord, which he will work for you today. . . ."* (Exod. 14:13 RSV).[4]

Jack Ensign Addington's book, *The Hidden Mystery of the Bible:*

> The Red Sea stands for race consciousness, those fixed beliefs of reality in evil that are ever with us in

our journey to the freedom of the Promised Land. Before we can pass through to the other side, the divine Law must divide the water of race consciousness. The Power of the Spirit makes the way clear to let the spiritual thinking through. The final barrier that each one must overcome is a Red Sea to him. It is the barrier of, *What will other people think? Is this the smart thing to do? Am I making a big mistake? If it's going around, I'll get it! Business is poor these days.*

Pharaoh was so sure that the Red Sea would stop them that he took after them to bring them back into slavery. And so it is with us as we go through that last period of rationalizing with erroneous thinking, that point when we say to ourselves, *maybe I have been too idealistic, maybe there is power in germs, maybe there is power in matter after all. . . .*

Isn't this what we all do when the going gets rough? Sometimes we think it would be easier to go back into our old bondage and make peace with negative thinking. Sometimes when we find ourselves *between the devil and the deep blue sea,* we are tempted to wonder if the battle is worth it. And then, the Moses in us, that strong spiritual thought that leads us out of our old negative patterns, tells us, "Fear not, stand firm, and see the salvation of the Lord."[5]

• **Think about how these states of consciousness might correspond to events in your own life (i.e., healing of illness, conquering financial problems, dealing with persecution, feeling an overwhelming sense of joy, etc.):** This story reminds me of all those times I have allowed myself to return to old, external-oriented thinking in the face of challenging circumstances.

- **Utilize the many interpretive lenses (i.e., factual, historical, dramatic, comedic, etc.):** This story is full of high drama. Moses and God had finally persuaded Pharaoh to let the Israelites leave Egypt, having resorted to the killing of all firstborn Egyptians. Pharaoh had second thoughts about his decision and sent his army out to stop them. The Israelites were caught between the sea and the army. Emotions must have been running high on both sides. Also, imagine how the Israelites felt walking through the corridor of dry ground with walls of water looming over them and the Egyptian chariots nipping at their heels.
- **Explore common metaphysical themes (i.e., illumination, healing, prosperity, etc.) as they might apply:** Faith in possibilities in the face of overwhelmingly pessimistic conditions.
- **Apply your own innate creative intelligence—look at the story from many vantage points and perspectives:** Let us focus on the reason for the whole predicament in the first place—water, and lots of it. Water is such a potent force in the Bible's history. It is the great equalizer. If it's on your side, you win. If not, you become swallowed up like the Egyptian army.

  Consider the Great Flood of Noah's era and the consequences it had for humanity and the earth.[6] Before the Red Sea encounter, Moses turned the waters of Egypt into blood, rendering them undrinkable. Later, Joshua and the Israelites, in a moment of déjà vu, crossed the Jordan River without even getting their sandals wet?[7] Almost any discussion of water and the Bible must include Jonah and his nautical adventures on the way to Nineveh[8] as well as Jesus' stroll on the Sea of Galilee.[9]
- **Remember, the metaphysical interpretive lens has an allegorical, psychological, and spiritual dimension:** Moses, Pharaoh, the Israelites, and the Egyptians must be looked at not just as historical figures but as aspects of our

own psyche. STEP THREE has helped us identify what they symbolize within us.

- **Finally, ask yourself, what jumps out at you about the passage. What clicks in you when you read it? Look for the personal, spiritual dimension that rises to the surface of your mind:** How frustrating it is when you feel you've finally become free of some old, unwanted thing, be it a habit or a relationship, only to have it re-enter your life and appear to once again block your good.

- **Write down your interpretation as soon as it is revealed to you:** This story is about transitions, going from one episode of life to another. Some transitions are easy, painless, and without conflict. Others are more difficult, requiring extraordinary strength and faith on our part. The transition illustrated by the Red Sea crossing is among the latter group.

     In this story, the Israelites are coming of age spiritually as a people. Initially, they lived as nomads during the time of the Patriarchs.[10] Later, they entered Egypt in great need and found help from one of their own—Joseph. They prospered for a while. After a period of time, they slipped into a state of bondage, serving as slaves to their Egyptian task masters for hundreds of years. It was time for them to grow up and move forward toward inheriting and inhabiting the land promised to them by God.

     However, they had become comfortable in their servitude, with enough to eat and a roof over their heads. They had to be pried away from their enslavement as much as the Pharaoh had to relax his grip on them. If they were to fulfill their spiritual destiny, they had to leave their comfort zone in Egypt. They didn't know they had to leave. This insight had to be revealed to them by God through his servant Moses. Their flight from Egypt and their encounter with the Red Sea challenged them spiritually, but it was a necessary step in their development of a consciousness able to overcome the odds that faced them ahead. Hence, the Exodus began as it did, with a spiritual lesson.

Metaphysically, we are the Israelites. We roam around for a while learning about life through trial and error, getting help when we need it (Patriarchal period). Eventually we discover material wealth (Egypt) and become attached (enslaved) to it. We become comfortable even though we're stuck in a rut, a cycle of serving the material world for the sake of it (i.e., dead-end job, tons of bills to pay, no end in sight).

> **"May mercy, peace, and love be yours in abundance."**
> —Jude 1:2

Along comes Moses (upward spiritual movement) and his message of freedom from the Egyptians (material consciousness). He represents that thought in our consciousness that draws us out (Hebrew meaning of Moses) of our self-imposed limitation (slavery). Moses (upward spiritual movement) tries everything in his bag of tricks (plagues) to get the Pharaoh (ruler of subconscious mind) to free the Israelites (you and me). This is a classic inner battle between the dark forces of the material (Egyptians) and the spiritual (The Lord) in the mind of humankind. It is a battle that the spiritual eventually wins, although it may take a long time (ten plagues) if the patient (Israelites) is deeply entrenched in materialistic thinking (hundreds of years of slavery).

Now, Moses and the Israelites are free and heading down the road to the Promised Land, and what do they come across but the Red Sea. And, to make things worse, who's hot on their trail? The Egyptian Army. Things aren't looking very good for Moses and his people.

The first step on the road to our spiritual freedom is often the most challenging. Subconscious memories of the comfort we once felt in materialism resurface (the appearance of the Egyptian Army) and try to reassert themselves (Pharaoh, ruler of the subconscious mind) by drawing us (Israelites) back in to old patterns of thinking (slavery in Egypt). The sea represents the mental unrest that we experience when materialistic thoughts recur. The Israelites (you and me) cry out (proclaim) their sorry case to Moses (upward spiritual movement), but he will not allow this state of mental agitation (sea) to block their journey. Moses (upward spiritual movement) reassures them (you and me) to stay their course and remain calm (see Exodus 14:14).

Now the real action begins. The Lord (spiritual nature) directs Moses (upward spiritual movement) to tell the Israelites (you and me) to advance toward the sea (mental unrest), but with an added instruction. This instruction is one of the most exciting moments in the Bible: "But you lift up your staff, and stretch out your hand over the sea and divide it, that the Israelites may go into the sea on dry ground."[11]

Moses (upward spiritual movement) lifts up (raises, exalts) his staff (spiritual authority and dominion) and stretches out (mental intention) his hand (ability to mentally grasp ideas) over the sea (mental unrest) and divides it (breaks apart) so that the Israelites (you and me) can go into the sea (through mental unrest) on dry ground (spiritual foundation without mental upheaval).

In the process of clearing the way for the Israelites, an angel of God appears (message of spiritual encouragement) along with a pillar of cloud (spiritual protection) that prevented the Egyptian Army (force of materialism) to come near the Israelites (you and me) all night (through our trials and soul searching). During the night a strong east wind (inner power and force) drives the sea (mental unrest) back, and the waters (thoughts of discouragement) are divided into walls (protection from upset). Then the Lord (spiritual nature) hardens (maintains momentarily) the hearts (feeling nature) of the Egyptians (material conscious-

> "Blessing and glory and wisdom and thanksgiving and honor and power and might be to our God forever and ever!"
> —Revelation 7:12

ness), and they pursue (persecute) them (you and me). Even though we make our way through the sea of unrest, our old thoughts chase us for a time, but not for long. The pillars of fire (spiritual illumination) and cloud (spiritual protection) look down (from high consciousness) upon the Egyptian Army (force of materialism) throwing them into a panic (fear of annihilation). The wheels (motive force) of the chariots (vehicles of consciousness) of the Egyptian Army (force of materialism) become clogged (without power) and turn with difficulty (not easy to operate without energy available). At this point the Egyptian Army (force of materialism) realizes it is fighting a losing battle and tries to escape its inevitable doom.

Here comes the next exciting moment, the destruction of the Egyptian Army, as the young boy in William Cameron's book put it, "Moses got on his walkie-talkie, called in the artillery, and blew them up." Well, not exactly. With the same movement of his arm that made the waters to stand on end, Moses (upward spiritual movement) causes the waters (undertow of negative thought) to return to their normal depth (permanent state) over the helpless Egyptians (material consciousness).

The Israelites (you and me) are saved (victorious) from (over) the Egyptians (material consciousness), and Israel (you and me) fears (reveres) the Lord (spiritual nature) and believes (trusts) the Lord (spiritual nature) and Moses (upward spiritual movement), his servant (that helps us).

The transition from materialistic outlook on life to a spiritual one is set into motion. There is no going back. Every experience hereafter must be approached with spiritual principle and consciousness. Henceforth, the rest of the Old Testament is an *autobiography* of the Israelite people and describes their successes and failures in living up to the spiritual meaning of the Exodus experience. This experience, although historically removed from our present-day life, is ours as well.

Notes

1. Exodus 14:15–31.

2. Acronym for *Metaphysical Bible Dictionary*.

3. Elizabeth Sand Turner, *Let There Be Light* (Unity Village, Mo.: Unity Books, 1996), p. 65.

4. William Earle Cameron, *Great Dramas of the Bible* (Unity Village, Mo.: Unity School of Christianity, 1984), p. 44.

5. Jack Ensign Addington, *The Hidden Mystery of the Bible* (New York: Dodd, Mead & Company, 1969), pp. 163–64.

6. Genesis 6–8.

7. Joshua 3:11–17.

8. Jonah 1–2.

9. Matthew 14:22–33, Mark 6:45–52, John 6:16–21.

10. Abraham through Isaac.

11. Exodus 14:16.

Appendix B

<u>Scriptural Fast Food</u>

Affirmations are an integral part of metaphysical Christian practice. These statements help to draw one's self from negative or mundane thinking into a positive, uplifting, and more rarefied state of mind. Affirmations take on an added dimension and power when they are derived from the Bible. We call these scriptural affirmations.

Scriptural affirmations are one- or two-line passages from the Bible that are easy to remember and personally relevant. We might call them "scriptural fast food" because we can quickly access them when the need arises. Write them down on index cards, post-it notes, or anywhere you can easily refer to them. Commit some to memory. Meditate on them during devotional time or whenever you have a free moment.

The following is a sample of scriptural fast food from each book of the Bible, including the Apocrypha, much of which is interspersed throughout the text of the book. All passages from the Old and New Testaments are from the New Revised Standard Version. Passages from the Apocrypha are from the New English Bible.

Hebrew Bible—Old Testament

Genesis 50:20—"Even though you intended to do harm to me, God intended it for good."

Exodus 15:2—"The Lord is my strength and my might."

Leviticus 26:9—"I will look with favor upon you and

make you fruitful and multiply you; and I will maintain my covenant with you."

Numbers 6:24–26—"The Lord bless you and keep you; the Lord make his face to shine upon you, and be gracious to you; the Lord lift up his countenance upon you, and give you peace."

Deuteronomy 6:5—"You shall love the Lord your God with all your heart, and with all your soul, and with all your might."

Joshua 1:8—"This book of the law shall not depart out of your mouth; you shall meditate on it day and night, so that you may be careful to act in accordance with all that is written in it. For then you shall make your way prosperous, and then you shall be successful."

Judges 5:31—"But may your friends be like the sun as it rises in its might."

Ruth 1:16—"Where you go, I will go; Where you lodge, I will lodge; your people shall be my people, and your God my God."

1 Samuel 2:2—"There is no Holy One like the Lord, no one besides you; there is no Rock like our God."

2 Samuel 7:3—"Go, do all that you have in mind; for the Lord is with you."

1 Kings 22:14—"As the Lord lives, whatever the Lord says to me, that I will speak."

2 Kings 6:27—"Let the Lord help you."

1 Chronicles 16:11—"Seek the Lord and his strength, seek his presence continually."

2 Chronicles 20:15—"The battle is not yours but God's."

Ezra 3:11—"For he is good, for his steadfast love endures forever."

Nehemiah 8:10—"The joy of the Lord is your strength."

Esther 5:3—"What is your request? It shall be given you."

Job 22:28—"You will decide on a matter, and it will be established for you, and light will shine on your ways."

Psalm 46:10—"Be still, and know that I am God!"

Proverbs 3:5—"Trust in the Lord with all your heart."

Ecclesiastes 3:1—"For everything there is a season, and a time for every matter under heaven."

Song of Solomon 4:7—"There is no flaw in you."

Isaiah 60:1—"Arise, shine; for your light has come, and the glory of the Lord has risen upon you."

Jeremiah 33:3—"Call to me and I will answer you, and will tell you great and hidden things that you have not known."

Lamentations 3:22—"The steadfast love of the Lord never ceases, his mercies never come to an end."

Ezekiel 36:26—"A new heart I will give you, and a new spirit I will put within you."

Daniel 10:19—"Do not fear, greatly beloved, you are safe. Be strong and courageous!"

Hosea 10:12—"Sow for yourselves righteousness; reap steadfast love; break up your fallow ground; for it is time to seek the Lord, that he may come and rain righteousness upon you."

Joel 2:26—"You shall eat in plenty and be satisfied, and praise the name of the Lord your God, who has dealt wondrously with you."

Amos 5:14—"Seek good and not evil, that you may live; and so the Lord, the God of hosts, will be with you, just as you have said."

Obadiah 1:15—"As you have done, it shall be done to you."

Jonah 2:2—"I called to the Lord out of my distress, and he answered me."

Micah 6:8—"He has told you, O mortal, what is good; and what does the Lord require of you but to do justice, and to love kindness, and to walk humbly with your God?"

Nahum 1:7—"The Lord is good, a stronghold in a day of trouble; he protects those who take refuge in him."

Habakkuk 2:20—"But the Lord is in his holy temple; let all the earth keep silence before him!"

Zephaniah 1:7—"Be silent before the Lord God! For the day of the Lord is at hand."

Haggai 2:19—"From this day on I will bless you."

Zechariah 8:16—"These are the things that you shall do: Speak the truth to one another, render in your gates judgments that are true and make for peace."

Malachi 3:10—"Bring the full tithe into the storehouse, so that there may be food in my house, and thus put me to the test, says the Lord of hosts; see if I will not open the windows of heaven for you and pour down for you an overflowing blessing."

Apocrypha

1 Esdras 4:40—"Praise be to the God of truth!"

2 Esdras 2:35—"Be ready to receive the rewards of the kingdom; for light perpetual will shine upon you for ever and ever."

Tobit 13:11—"Your light shall shine brightly to all the ends of the earth."

Judith 16:13—"O Lord, thou art great and glorious, thou art marvellous in thy strength, invincible."

Esther 7:2—"What is your request? What is your petition? You shall have it."

Wisdom of Solomon 6:17—"The true beginning of wisdom is the desire to learn."

Ecclesiasticus 39:33—"All the works of the Lord are good, and he supplies every need as it occurs."

Baruch 1:12—"So the Lord will give us strength, and light to walk by."

Letter of Jeremiah 1:7—"For my angel is with you; your lives are in his care."

Song of Three 1:35—"Let the whole creation bless the Lord, sing his praise and exalt him for ever."

Daniel and Susanna 1:60—"Then the whole assembly gave a great shout and praised God, the saviour of those who trust in him."

Daniel, Bel, and the Snake 1:25—"I will worship the Lord my God, for he is the living God."

Prayer of Manasseh 1:7—"For thou art Lord Most High, compassionate, patient, and of great mercy."

1 **Maccabees 3:19**—"Strength comes from Heaven alone."

2 **Maccabees 7:23**—"It is the Creator of the universe who moulds man at his birth and plans the origin of all things."

New Testament

Matthew 19:26—"For mortals it is impossible, but for God all things are possible."

Mark 5:34—"Your faith has made you well."

Luke 6:38—"Give, and it will be given to you. A good measure, pressed down, shaken together, running over, will be put into your lap; for the measure you give will be the measure you get back."

John 14:12—"Very truly, I tell you, the one who believes in me will also do the works that I do and, in fact, will do greater works than these."

Acts 17:28—"For 'In him we live and move and have our being'; as even some of your own poets have said, 'For we too are his offspring.'"

Romans 12:2—"Do not be conformed to this world, but be transformed by the renewing of your minds, so that you may discern what is the will of God—what is good and acceptable and perfect."

1 **Corinthians 14:1**—"Pursue love and strive for the spiritual gifts."

2 **Corinthians 6:16**—"For we are the temple of the living God."

Galatians 5:22–23—"The fruit of the Spirit is love, joy, peace, patience, kindness, generosity, faithfulness, gentleness, and self-control."

Ephesians 2:8—"For by grace you have been saved through faith, and this is not your own doing; it is the gift of God."

Philippians 4:6—"Do not worry about anything, but in

everything by prayer and supplication with thanksgiving let your requests be made known to God."

Colossians 1:27—"Christ in you, the hope of glory."

1 Thessalonians 5:16–18—"Rejoice always, pray without ceasing, give thanks in all circumstances."

2 Thessalonians 3:3—"But the Lord is faithful; he will strengthen you and guard you from the evil one."

1 Timothy 4:4—"For everything created by God is good."

2 Timothy 1:7—"For God did not give us a spirit of cowardice, but rather a spirit of power and of love and of self-discipline."

Titus 2:11—"For the grace of God has appeared, bringing salvation to all."

Philemon 1:4—"I always thank my God."

Hebrews 11:1—"Now faith is the assurance of things hoped for, the conviction of things not seen."

James 3:17—"But the wisdom from above is first pure, then peaceable, gentle, willing to yield, full of mercy and good fruits, without a trace of partiality or hypocrisy."

1 Peter 1:23—"You have been born anew, not of perishable but of imperishable seed, through the living and enduring word of God."

2 Peter 1:3—"His divine power has given us everything needed for life and godliness."

1 John 4:4—". . . the one who is in you is greater than the one who is in the world."

1 John 4:18—"There is no fear in love, but perfect love casts out fear."

2 John 1:5—"Let us love one another."

3 John 1:11—"Whoever does good is from God."

Jude 1:2—"May mercy, peace, and love be yours in abundance."

Revelation 7:12—"Blessing and glory and wisdom and thanksgiving and honor and power and might be to our God forever and ever!"

Bibliography

This bibliography includes books from my own Bible study library that I consulted for general background information as well as those quoted in *Wisdom for a Lifetime*. I have categorized the books by chapter, although some books are used in more than one chapter. Most of the older books are out of print but can be found in larger libraries.

Chapter 1—The Purpose of This Book

Aaseng, Rolf E. *A Beginner's Guide to Studying the Bible.* Augsburg Fortress: Minneapolis, 1991.

Grun, Bernard. *The Timetables of History.* New York: Simon & Schuster, 1979.

Hann, Robert R. *The Bible: An Owner's Manual.* Paulist Press: New York, 1983.

Johnson, Henry Lewis. *Gutenberg and the Book of Books.* New York: William Edwin Rudge, 1932.

Chapter 2—The Bible Is Not a Book

Friedman, Richard Elliott. *Who Wrote the Bible.* New York: Harper & Row, 1987.

Chapter 3—The Sacredness of Scripture

American Civil Religion. Russell E. Richey and Donald G. Jones (eds.). New York: Harper & Row, 1974.

The Analects of Confucius. Lionel Giles (trans.). New York: The Heritage Press, 1970.

Bhagavad Gita. Swami Nikhilananda (ed. and trans.). New York: Ramakrishna-Vivekananda Center, 1969.

Cady, H. Emilie. *Lessons in Truth.* Unity Village: Unity Books, 1903.

The Dhammapada. P. Lal. (trans.). New York: Noonday Press, 1967.

Eddy, Mary Baker. *Science and Health.* 1875; rpt. Boston: The First Church of Christ Science, 1934.

The Koran. N. J. Dawood (trans.). 1956; rpt. Middlesex: Penguin Books, 1974.

Narayan, R. K. *The Mahabharata.* New York: Viking Press, 1978.

Pangborn, Cyrus R. *Zoroastrianism—A Beleagured Faith.* New York: Advent Books, 1983.

The Portable World Bible. Robert O. Ballou (ed.). 1944; rpt. New York: Penguin Books, 1976.

Tao Te Ching. Gia-Fu Feng and Jane English (trans.). New York: Vintage Books, 1972.

The Upanishads. Swami Nikhilananda (ed. and trans.). 1963; rpt. New York: Harper & Row, 1964.

Chapter 4—Metaphysical Christianity's Biblical Heritage

Butterworth, Eric. *Discover the Power Within You.* New York: Harper & Row, 1968.

———, *Metamorality.* Unity Village: Unity Books, 1988.

Cameron, William Earle. *Great Dramas of the Bible.* Unity Village: Unity School of Christianity, 1982.

Fillmore, Charles. *Mysteries of Genesis.* Unity Village: Unity School of Christianity, 1989.

———, *Mysteries of John.* Unity Village: Unity School of Christianity, 1946.

Fox, Emmet. *The Sermon on the Mount.* New York: HarperCollins, 1938.

Hasbrouck, Hypatia. *The Trip to Bethlehem.* Seattle: Peanut Butter Publishing, 1995.

Metaphysical Bible Dictionary. Unity Village: Unity School of Christianity, 1931.

Neal, Charles A. *Revelation: The Road to Overcoming.* Unity Village: Unity School of Christianity, 1990.

Paulson, Sig, and Ric Dickerson. *Revelation: The Book of Unity.* 1976; rpt. Unity Village: Unity School of Christianity, 1981.

Ponder, Catherine. *The Millionaire From Nazareth.* Marina del Rey: DeVORSS & Co., 1979.

Turner, Elizabeth Sand. *Be Ye Transformed.* Unity Village: Unity School of Christianity, 1969.

————, *Let There Be Light.* Unity Village: Unity School of Christianity, 1954.

————, *Your Hope of Glory.* Unity Village: Unity School of Christianity, 1959.

West, Georgiana Tree. *Prosperity's Ten Commandments.* Unity Village: Unity Books, 1996.

Wilson, Ernest C. *The Week That Changed the World.* Unity Village: Unity School of Christianity, 1990.

Chapter 5—Getting Started

Beegle, Dewey M. *God's Word Into English.* Grand Rapids: William B. Eerdmans Publishing Co., 1960.

Bruce, F.F. *History of the Bible in English.* New York: Oxford University Press, 1978.

Butterworth, Charles C. *The Literary Lineage of the King James Bible.* Philadelphia: University of Pennsylvania Press, 1941.

Hunting, Harold B. *The Story of Our Bible.* New York: Charles Scribner's Sons, 1915.

MacGregor, Geddes. *A Literary History of the Bible.* Nashville: Abingdon Press, 1968.

Price, Ira Maurice. *The Ancestry of Our English Bible*, (2d ed). Philadelphia: The Sunday School Times Company, 1907.

Chapter 6—Making a Bible Study Tool Kit

Alexander, David, and Pat Alexander (eds.). *Eerdmans' Handbook to the Bible.* Grand Rapids: Eerdmans, 1974.

Anderson, Bernhard W. *Understanding the Old Testament.* Englewood Cliffs: Prentice-Hall, 1975.

Barthel, Manfred. *What the Bible Really Says.* New York: Quill, 1983.

Blair, Edward P. *Abingdon Bible Handbook.* Nashville: Abingdon, 1975.

Bryant, T. Alton (ed.). *The New Compact Bible Dictionary.* Grand Rapids: Zondervan, 1979.

Buttrick, George Arthur et al., *The Interpreter's Bible.* 12 vols. Nashville: Abingdon, 1982.

———, *The Interpreter's Dictionary of the Bible.* 5 vols. Nashville: Abingdon, 1982.

Cruden, Alexander. *Cruden's Complete Concordance.* C. H. Irwin, A. D. Adams, and S. A. Waters (eds.). Guildford: Lutterworth Press, 1982.

Davis, John D. *A Dictionary of the Bible.* Philadelphia: Westminster Press, 1942.

Gannt, Michael. *A Non-Churchgoer's Guide to the Bible.* Intercourse: Good Books, 1995.

Hendricks, Howard G. and William D. *Living by the Book.* Chicago: Moody Press, 1991.

Josephus, Flavius. *The Works of Flavius Josephus.* William Whiston (trans.). 4 vols. Grand Rapids: Baker, 1982.

Laymon, Charles M., (ed.). *The Interpreter's One-Volume Commentary on the Bible.* Nashville: Abingdon, 1980.

May, Herbert G. et al., (eds.). *Oxford Bible Atlas.* New York: Oxford University Press, 1985.

Metzger, Bruce M., and Michael D. Coogan (eds.). *The Oxford Companion to the Bible.* New York: Oxford University Press, 1993.

Peloubet, F. N., and Alice D. Adams (eds.). *Peloubet's Bible Dictionary.* Philadelphia: John C. Winston Company, 1947.

Reader's Digest. *Atlas of the Bible.* Pleasantville, New York: Reader's Digest, 1981.

———, *Great People of the Bible and How They Live.* Pleasantville, New York: Reader's Digest, 1974.

———, *Mysteries of the Bible.* Pleasantville, New York: Reader's Digest, 1988.

Riedel, Eunice et al. *The Book of the Bible.* New York: Bantam, 1981.

Strong, James. *Strong's Exhaustive Concordance of the Bible.*

Chapter 7—Close to the Source

Aland, Kurt, et al., *The Greek New Testament.* New York: United Bible Societies, 1975.

Crosby, Henry Lamar, and John Nevin Schaeffer. *An Introduction to Greek.* Boston: Allyn and Bacon, 1928.

Davies, A. Powell. *The Meaning of the Dead Sea Scrolls.* New American Library: New York, 1956.

Gesenius' Hebrew-Chaldee Lexicon to the Old Testament. Samuel Prideaux Tregelles (trans.). Grand Rapids: Baker, 1979.

Greek-English Lexicon of the New Testament. Joseph Henry Thayer (trans.). Grand Rapids: Zondervan, 1979.

LaSor, William Sanford. *Amazing Dead Sea Scrolls.* Chicago: Moody Press, 1956.

The NIV Triglot Old Testament. Grand Rapids: Zondervan, 1981.

Shanks, Herschel, et al. *The Dead Sea Scrolls After Forty Years.* Washington: Biblical Archaeological Society, 1991.

Vaughan, Curtis, and Virtus E. Gideon. *A Greek Grammar of the New Testament.* Nashville: Broadman, 1979.

Weingreen, J. *A Practical Grammar for Classical Hebrew.* New York: 1959.

Chapter 8—Everyone Interprets the Bible

Hasbrouck, Hypatia. *Handbook of Positive Prayer*. Unity Village: Unity Books, 1995.

Ohlsen, Woodrow. *Perspectives on Old Testament Literature*. New York: Harcourt, 1979.

Chapter 9—The Uniqueness of Metaphysical Interpretation

Addington, Jack Ensign. *The Hidden Mystery of the Bible*. New York: Dodd, Mead & Company, 1969.

Fillmore, Charles. *Keep a True Lent*. Unity Village: Unity Books, 1995.

Johnston, William (ed. and trans.). *The Cloud of Unknowing*. Garden City: Image Books, 1973.

Chapter 10—Obtaining the Most From Your Bible

Funk, Robert, et al. *The Five Gospels*. New York: Macmillan, 1993.

Gregory, Dick. *Dick Gregory's Bible Tales*. New York: Harper & Row, 1978.

Harron, Don. *Olde Charlie Farquharson's Testament*. Toronto: Macmillan of Canada, 1978.

Glossary

Aesop—Ancient Greek storyteller, sixth century B.C.E.

ASV—American Standard Version, 1901 C.E.

Analects—Writings of Confucius

Anglo-Saxon—Old English, language of England, c. 500–1100 C.E.

Apocalyptic—Belonging to those prophetic writings describing the battle between good and evil and ultimate triumph of good over evil

Apocrypha—Term used to describe those writings of both Jewish and Christian origins that were not included in the sixty-six books of the Bible. Some of the Jewish books are included in Catholic Bibles.

Aramaic—Ancient language of Palestine, akin to Hebrew, the language of Jesus

Authorized Version—A.V., same as King James Version, KJV

B.C.E.—Before the Common Era, formerly B.C.

Bhagavad Gita—Hindu scripture, part of the *Mahabharata* epic, sixth century B.C.E.

Bible Atlas—Atlas used to locate places mentioned in the Bible

Bible Commentary—Book of scholarly information and interpretations of the Bible

Bible Concordance—Book used to locate words in the Bible

Bible Dictionary—Book used to define subject matter in the Bible

Bible Handbook—Concise book used to gain general information about the Bible

Book of Mormon—Scripture of the Mormon church, 1830 C.E.

Buddha—Also known as Siddhartha Gautama, founder of Buddhism, sixth century B.C.E.

Buddhism—Religion originated in India, practiced today in many Asian countries

Bundahis—Scripture of Zoroastrianism

H. Emilie Cady—Homeopathic physician, 1848–1941 C.E., whose book *Lessons in Truth* was first book published by Unity School of Christianity in 1903

John Calvin—Early reformer of Christian church, sixteenth century C.E.

Canaanites—Ancient indigenous people of Palestine

Canon—Refers to those writings considered authoritative and thus included in the Bible

C.E.—Common Era, formerly A.D.

CEV—Contemporary English Version, 1995 C.E.

Christian Science—Church founded by Mary Baker Eddy, headquartered in Boston, Massachusetts, began 1875 C.E.

Cloud of Unknowing—Book of contemplative ideas by an unknown English writer, fourteenth century C.E.

Confucius—Also known as K'ung Fu-tzu, philosopher whose ideas strongly affected Chinese culture, sixth century B.C.E.

Alexander Cruden—Published English Bible concordance in 1737 C.E.

Dead Sea Scrolls—Ancient manuscripts, including portions of the Hebrew Bible, found in a cave near the Dead Sea in 1947 C.E.

Deuteronomic Historian—Literary source of Old Testament, also known as the D writer, emphasized the importance of religious law, 621–561 B.C.E.

Dhammapada—Buddhist scripture, written in Pali

Douay-Rheims—Early Catholic English translation of the Bible, 1609 C.E.

Ecclesiastical—Relating to church and religious organizations

Mary Baker Eddy—Founder of the Christian Science Church, author of *Science and Health,* 1821–1910 C.E.

Elohist—Literary source of Old Testament, also known as the E writer, used the word *Elohim* for God, *c.* 850 B.C.E.

English Revised Version—English revision of the King James Version, 1870 C.E.

Epistle—Letter, pertaining to New Testaments letters

Exegesis—Interpretative process of analyzing the original words of the Bible

Exile—Refers to the period of captivity many Jews endured at the hands of the Babylonians, having been transported to Babylon during this period, 597–538 B.C.E.

Galilean—An inhabitant of Galilee, a region adjacent to the Sea of Galilee

Charles Fillmore—Co-founder of Unity School of Christianity, author of several Bible interpretation books, 1854–1948 C.E.

Emmet Fox—Metaphysical Christian author, d. 1951 C.E.

Greek—Ancient language of the New Testament

Gutenberg Bible—First Bible printed on a press, 1455 C.E.

Hebrew—Ancient language of the Hebrew Bible/Old Testament

Hebrew Bible—Old Testament

Hinduism—Believed to be the oldest of the world religions, primarily practiced today in India, Sri Lanka, and Bali

Iliad & Odyssey—Greek epic poems attributed to Homer, seventh century B.C.E.

Indo-European—Group of languages that include most European as well as some south Asian languages, including English, German, Greek, Armenian, and Hindi to name a few

Interpretive Lens—Mental filter through which we view life

Islam—Believed to be the youngest of the world religions, originated in Arabia, now practiced worldwide

Jahwist—Literary source of Old Testament, also known as the J writer, used word *Yahweh* for God, 950 B.C.E.

Jehovah—European transliteration of the Hebrew YHWH

Jericho—Most ancient city in the world, archaeology dates it to 7000 B.C.E.

Jerusalem Bible—Catholic English translation of the Bible, 1966 C.E.

Jewish Publication Society of America—Published English translation of Hebrew Bible, 1917–1982 C.E.

Johannes Gutenberg—Inventor of the printing press

Judeo-Christian—Relating to both Jewish and Christian ideals and traditions, including historical roots

KJV—King James Version, 1611 C.E.

Koran—Scripture of Islam, also known as the Qur'an, seventh century C.E.

Lamsa Bible—English Bible translation of Peshitta by George Lamsa, 1957 C.E.

George Lamsa—English Bible scholar from Kurdistan, translated Peshitta into English

Lao Tzu—Writer of the *Tao-te Ching*, sixth century B.C.E.

Latin Vulgate—Latin translation of the Bible by St. Jerome, *c.* 400 C.E.

Lessons in Truth—First book published by Unity School of Christianity, written by H. Emilie Cady, 1903 C.E.

Mahabharata—World's longest epic poem, contains the Hindu scripture, *Bhagavad Gita,* 500 B.C.E.

John Marbeck—Published first English Bible concordance in 1550 C.E.

Martin Luther—Founder of the Protestant Reformation in sixteenth century C.E., translated the Bible into German

Masoretic Text—Known as the MT, Hebrew Old Testament manuscript, tenth century C.E.

Metaphysical—Literally meaning "beyond the physical," pertains to the study of spiritual principles and phenomena

Metaphysical Bible Dictionary—Published by Unity School of Christianity in 1931 C.E., presents interpretations of biblical characters, places, and objects

Metaphysical Christianity—Branch of Christianity that includes movements such as Unity, Religious Science, Divine Science, and New Thought

Middle English—Language of England *c.* 1100–1500 C.E.

Modernize—To make a story more relevant by retelling it as if it happened today

Mormon—Also known as the Church of Jesus Christ of Latter-day Saints, headquartered in Salt Lake City, Utah, founded by Joseph Smith in 1830 C.E.

Muhammed—Founder of Islam, writer of the Koran, seventh century C.E.

NASB—New American Standard Bible, 1971 C.E.

National Enquirer—Sensational American tabloid newspaper

NEB—New English Bible, 1970 C.E.

New Thought—Spiritual movement that began in the mid to late nineteenth century C.E. that emphasizes the importance of the mind in creating tangible results

NIV—New International Version, 1978 C.E.

NKJV—New King James Version, 1982 C.E.

NRSV—New Revised Standard Version, 1989 C.E.

Parsis—Modern-day adherents of Zoroastrian religion, name derived from homeland of Persia

Passover—Jewish holiday celebrated in memory of the final plague God brought upon the Egyptians that led to Israelite deliverance from slavery

Pentateuch—First five books of the Bible, attributed to Moses

Peshitta—Bible of the Syrian Christians considered to be the first translation of the entire Bible into the vernacular, *c.* 150 C.E.

J. B. Phillips—English Bible translator

Phillips Modern English Bible—Translation of the New Testament by J. B. Phillips, 1947–72 C.E.

Priestly Writer—A literary source of the Old Testament, emerged from the Jewish priests concerned with adherence to rituals and traditions, *c.* 550 B.C.E.

Promised Land—Refers to the region of Palestine promised by God to Abraham

Protestant Reformation—Religious movement that broke with the Christian (Catholic) church in Rome, began early sixteenth century C.E.

Reader's Digest Bible—Paraphrase of the Revised Standard Version

Qumran—Ruins of ancient religious community located near discovery of the Dead Sea Scrolls

REB—Revised English Bible, 1989 C.E.

RSV—Revised Standard Version, 1952 C.E.

Semitic—Middle Eastern group of languages that include Arabic, Aramaic, Canaanite, and Hebrew

Septuagint—Greek translation of the Hebrew Bible, third century B.C.E.

SV—Scholar's Version, translated by the Jesus Seminar, 1985–1993 C.E.

James Strong—Published English Bible concordance in 1890 C.E., still widely used today

Syriac—Middle Eastern language similar to Aramaic, language of the Peshitta

Tao-te Ching—Scripture of Taoism, sixth century B.C.E.

TEV—Today's English Version, also known as the Good News Bible, 1976 C.E.

Torah—First five books of the Old Testament

Unity School of Christianity—Metaphysical Christian church founded by Charles and Myrtle Fillmore, headquartered at Unity Village, Missouri, near Kansas City, began in 1889 C.E.

Upanishads—Collection of Hindu scriptures, philosophical part of the Vedas, 800–500 B.C.E.

Transliteration—Rendering a word from one language to another in the latter's alphabet

William Tyndale—Father and martyr of English Bible translation, 1492–1536 C.E.

Vedas—Most ancient and authoritative of Hindu scriptures, written in Sanskrit, includes the Upanishads, 1500–500 B.C.E.

Vernacular—Native language

John Wycliffe—Translated the Bible into Middle English, 1320–1384 C.E.

YHWH—Refers to the unutterable Hebrew word for God, Yahweh, Jehovah, usually translated as Lord

Zoroaster—Also known as Zarathustra, founder of a religion that dominated Persia until advent of Islam, seventh century B.C.E.

Zoroastrianism—Ancient religion of Persia, practiced today by the Parsis in Bombay region of India

Permissions

Excerpts from The Jerusalem Bible, copyright © 1966 by Darton, Longman & Todd, Ltd. and Doubleday, a division of Bantam Doubleday Dell Publishing Group, Inc. Reprinted by permission.

Excerpts from The Holy Bible—New Revised Standard Version, copyright © 1972 by Thomas Nelson Inc., are reprinted by permission.

Excerpts from the New English Bible, copyright © 1961, 1970 and Revised English Bible, copyright © 1989, by Oxford University Press and Cambridge University Press, are reprinted by permission.

Scripture taken from the New American Standard Bible (R), © Copyright The Lockman Foundation 1960, 1962, 1963, 1968, 1971, 1972, 1973, 1975, 1977. Used by permission.

Scripture quotations identified as TEV are taken from the Today's English Version, Second Edition Copyright © 1966, 1971, 1976, 1992 by American Bible Society. Used by permission.

Scripture taken from the Holy Bible, New International Version (R). NIV (R). Copyright © 1973, 1978, 1984 by International Bible Society. Used by permission of Zondervan Publishing House. All rights reserved.

Scripture quotations identified as CEV are taken from the Contemporary English Version © 1991, 1992, 1995 by American Bible Society. Used by permission.

Excerpts from The Writings—Kethubim, copyright © 1982,

Index

About the Author

The Reverend Alden Henry Studebaker, Jr., is the senior minister at Garden Park Unity Church in Cincinnati, Ohio. He conducts seminars and workshops on Bible usage and interpretation throughout the country.

Alden was born on February 19, 1957, in East Chicago, Indiana, and lived in the small town of Dune Acres on the shore of Lake Michigan. At the age of ten, his family moved to Honolulu, Hawaii. In 1971 Alden's family began attending a Unity church, and he soon became involved with the Youth of Unity (Y.O.U.), serving as its president and attending the Y.O.U. international conferences at Unity Village, Missouri, in 1973 and 1975.

Alden enrolled as a chemistry major at the University of Hawaii. While attending college, he began to question his career track. One Sunday, while listening to a minister's message, he received his call to the ministry. He returned to the continental United States and entered Western Michigan University in Kalamazoo, Michigan. It was there that he began to study the Bible extensively, including courses in Greek, Latin and Hebrew. Alden received a Bachelor of Arts degree, magna cum laude, in 1980, graduating with a major in religion and a minor in history.

Studebaker was ordained in 1984 after graduating from the Unity Ministerial School at Unity Village. He has served Unity churches in Vacaville, California; El Paso, Texas; La Crescenta, California; and Bellevue, Washington, before moving to Cincinnati.

Alden Studebaker lives on five acres in Bright, Indiana, with his wife Donna, a licensed Unity teacher, and their three children, Jennifer, Nathan, and Danny.

Recommended in *Wisdom For A Lifetime* as a Key Component in your Bible Study Tool Kit.

Metaphysical Bible Dictionary
by Charles Fillmore

"Contained within the more than 700 pages of this book are definitions for every person and place mentioned in the Bible and its metaphysical interpretation. It is an awesome piece of work and required many years to complete. Read by people throughout the metaphysical Christian world, **there is nothing else like it.** The *Metaphysical Bible Dictionary* stands alone as the standard and is a must for any serious Bible student."

> —Alden Studebaker, author of *Wisdom for a Lifetime: How to Get the Bible Off the Shelf and Into Your Hands,* Chapter 4, "Metaphysical Christianity's Biblical Heritage," p. 53

This current edition from the Charles Fillmore Reference Library, released in 1995, is a one-of-a-kind volume presenting the metaphysical meanings of names and people, places, key words, and phrases found in the Bible. Open up new avenues of thought through the ideas presented in this unique Bible reference book.

ISBN 0-87159-067-0 $19.95, hardcover   Size: 7" x 10 1/4", 706 pp.
Features: Gold engraving, library nameplate page, unique endpaper

To order: ❏ Check   ❏ Money Order   ❏ MasterCard   ❏ Visa
Payment must accompany order. Sorry, no COD.
Overseas customers, your payment must be in U.S. funds.

To charge by phone, call **(816) 969-2069 or 1-800-669-0282 or Fax (816) 251-3554**
For Wholesale orders: **(816) 251-3571 or Fax (816) 251-3551**

Or mail order form to: Unity Books and Multimedia Publishing
1901 NW Blue Parkway
Unity Village, MO 64065-0001

Item #	Title	Price	Qty.	Total
#78	Metaphysical Bible Dictionary	$19.95		

Subtotal $_____
Postage and handling $_____
TOTAL $_____

Humankind Stands Between the Lightning and the Thunder . . . Stands in the Present and the Future, Poised to Co-Create With God the World As It Can Be

New Thought for a New Millennium
Twelve Powers for the 21st Century
Edited with an Introduction by Michael A. Maday

"I believe that New Thought Christianity will be a hugely significant force in the twenty-first century."

> —Marianne Williamson, author of *A Return to Love, A Woman's Worth, Illuminata,* and *The Healing of America*

"Reading *New Thought for a New Millennium* I imagined twelve great sages gathered in a room discussing their positive visions of the future . . . it was an awesome feeling. As I completed the book I felt I had experienced something extraordinary."

> —John Randolph Price, best-selling author and chairman of the Quartus Foundation

New Thought for a New Millennium is an alternate Spring selection of ONE SPIRIT BOOK CLUB and is found in fine bookstores everywhere. Authors Sir John Templeton, Bernie Siegel, M.D., Barbara Marx Hubbard, Eric Butterworth, James Dillet Freeman, Joan Gattuso, Christopher Jackson, Jim Rosemergy, Robert Brumet, Rosemary Ellen Guiley, Barbara King, and Rosemary Fillmore Rhea write with great depth and consciousness to create a compendium of thought guaranteed to be a best-seller.

ISBN 0-87159-205-3 $19.95, hardcover   Size: 6 1/8" x 9 1/4", 256 pp.
ISBN 0-87159-837-X $27.95, four cassettes (abridged audiobook)

To order: ❏ Check   ❏ Money Order   ❏ MasterCard   ❏ Visa
Payment must accompany order. Sorry, no COD.
Overseas customers, your payment must be in U.S. funds.

To charge by phone, call **(816) 969-2069 or 1-800-669-0282 or Fax (816) 251-3554**
For Wholesale orders: **(816) 251-3571 or Fax (816) 251-3551**

Or mail order form to: Unity Books and Multimedia Publishing
1901 NW Blue Parkway
Unity Village, MO 64065-0001

Item #	Title	Price	Qty.	Total
#1	New Thought for a New Millennium	$19.95		
#7425	New Thought for a New Millennium Audiobook	$27.95		

Subtotal $_____
Postage and handling $_____
TOTAL $_____

Printed U.S.A.

51-3841-15M-3-98